STORECUPBOARD

One Pound Meals

PHOTOGRAPHY
DAN JONES

DESIGN
SUPERFANTASTIC

STORECUPBOARD

One Pound Meals

CONTENTS

Here's a list of all the recipes in the book.
Simply see what's in your kitchen cupboard and take your pick.

WELCOME

I feel so lucky to be writing my sixth book; it's a real honour and I can't thank you guys enough for all the support you've given me over the past few years. It has been a strange experience writing during lockdown, with limited food on the shelves and a nation changing the way it thinks about what it eats. This book has been shaped by what is currently going on. I had to use what was available in my own storecupboard, and it felt great to finally use it all up! I enjoyed the challenge of making the best use of what I already had – pastas, tins, jars, grains and frozen food – and this book became more like a handbook for a new era of cooking in the world we are now living in.

We've all got items in the storecupboard saved away for a rainy day, and perhaps we feel a little uninspired by what to do with them – after all, there are always more glamorous ingredients vying for our attention on the supermarket shelves. But now is the time to get in the kitchen, to feel inspired to cook in a new way, using storecupboard ingredients as the main focus of our meals.

Miguel

MIGUEL'S
STORECUPBOARD ESSENTIALS

Bacon: so delicious and lasts for ages because it's cured. Its concentrated flavour lends itself well to the One Pound Meals 'a little goes a long way' philosophy. Chuck a tiny bit into a pasta dish and it will be packed with flavour.

Breadcrumbs: great for adding texture to a dish as a quick topping, or for coating things like fishcakes to make them extra delicious. I always keep any leftover bread, let it go stale and then blitz it into breadcrumbs.

Cannellini beans: a staple storecupboard ingredient – I'd be lost without them. They're great for bulking out a meal and keep things classy in a provincial Italian way (Italian is my favourite cuisine).

Chickpeas: probably the first food that came to mind when I thought of storecupboard ingredients. Chickpeas are one of my all-time favourite One Pound Meal ingredients. I love roasting them in the oven to give a little bit of crunch and texture to a dish. They are super versatile and take on flavour well.

Chopped tomatoes: the king of storecupboard ingredients. I like the fact that they're not too processed and still taste fresh, but give a different result from fresh tomatoes. An essential ingredient for all those tasty Italian tomato-based sauces.

Chorizo: when I first started cooking my One Pound Meals, this was my number-one ingredient. It provides unparalleled amounts of flavour with those paprika-infused oils, and if you can manage to get a little charring on the outside, you can double the intensity of flavour. Another 'a little goes a long way' ingredient that is definitely in my top ten for cooking tasty food on a budget.

Coconut milk: transforms your curries by giving them that authentic Thai flavour. It's the secret ingredient to getting a smooth, creamy texture.

Couscous: another inexpensive ingredient to bulk out a meal, and it tastes great too. My shortcut is to add it to whatever you're cooking along with a splash of water and it'll plump up while absorbing flavour.

Cumin: a classic spice that I use a lot in my Mexican cooking. A teaspoon of ground cumin will impart a warm, earthy flavour to everything from soups and stews to marinades and rubs.

Curry powder: way less hassle than keeping a huge selection of different spices, and cheaper too. There are so many blends out there, it's fun to experiment to keep things interesting. Curry powder is a helpful shortcut to maximum flavour.

Feta: tangy and salty, a little of this cheese goes a long way. It's a key ingredient in some great Greek dishes. Try crumbling it onto a salad to create a more substantial meal.

Flour: mega versatile, used for making all sorts of doughs, for thickening sauces and binding ingredients together, like in my Cheesy Veggie Balls recipe (see page 138). Flour is truly the definition of a storecupboard essential.

Frozen fish: I buy loads of frozen fish, as it's cheaper and often fresher than fresh fish. The clock is always ticking with fish and it can be difficult to know how fresh it really is when it's filleted and packed in plastic.

Frozen pastry: pies and tarts maximise your ingredients and stretch them further – plus anything in pastry is tasty. When it comes to puff pastry, don't bother making it yourself, just buy it ready-made. I promise you'll be saving yourself a lot of effort.

Frozen prawns: luxurious and decadent, you might expect prawns to be expensive, but have a look in the frozen aisle and you'll see they are cheaper than you think. I love the fact that you can just take a handful out of the bag to create beautiful pasta, noodle or rice dishes without having to defrost them. If you want to eat posh on a budget, frozen prawns are the way to do it.

Frozen spinach: a phenomenon! It's crazy what good value frozen spinach is. What's more, you can chuck some into a dish at a moment's notice and the rest of the bag is kept safe in the freezer for another day with no waste.

Frozen veg: great for chucking into curries, stews and fried rice, and adds both colour and vibrancy to your cooking. One of the best ways to avoid waste, as you can just dip into the bag and take what you need.

Noodles: a quick and easy way to turn a few leftovers into a full meal. Rice noodles in particular are ready in seconds – just dip them in boiling water.

Olive oil: a versatile oil that I use in all my cooking – yes, even when I make a curry. I like a simple life and having one bottle of oil by the stove makes my life easier.

Oregano: get a real Italian flavour with a pinch of oregano. It's great in tomato sauces and is a key flavour in New York pizzas. It's definitely my most used herb – I buy it in huge bags! Oregano is one of those herbs that is actually better dried than fresh, so take advantage and keep some in your storecupboard.

Orzo: a cross between rice and pasta. I always have a pack in my cupboard. What I love most about orzo is that you don't necessarily need to boil it in a pan; it's so small you can just chuck it into whatever you're cooking with some extra water and create amazing one-pot dishes in minutes.

Paprika: has a beautiful smoky flavour that is unmistakable. A little goes a long way and provides an extra dimension to your cooking by immediately adding all those flavours that usually take time to develop.

Pesto: another cheat's ingredient I've leaned on for this storecupboard book. Pesto lasts for such a long time that you might as well have some to hand for a rainy day. Just a spoonful can make a plain dish like pasta taste spectacular.

Rice: the perfect ingredient to bulk out a dish. It costs pennies and is a delicious food that you can cook from scratch really easily. I love the smell and flavour of freshly cooked rice, and I always cook a little more than I need so I can make fried rice with the leftovers.

Roasted red peppers (in a jar): not just an antipasto; try using them in salads and pastas. They have already been cooked and keep for ages, so they're minimum hassle.

Salt & pepper: the cornerstones of cookery, these will enhance the natural flavour of your ingredients and let them shine through. Take the humble chip – it just tastes better with salt.

Sausages: you never have to worry about flavour with sausages, they're already packed with it! They're a great cheat ingredient. I like to make them go further by chopping them into small chunks and bulking them out with other ingredients to create tasty meals.

Soy sauce: an essential part of any East Asian cuisine. It adds a depth of flavour and saltiness to bring your dish closer to that authentic taste you're searching for.

Stock cubes: making stock is simply not viable when you are time-poor or unprepared. That's where stock cubes come in. Instant stock is the stuff of dreams, because without it there would be no weeknight risottos or quick stews.

Thai green curry paste: a cheat's ingredient that's well worth buying. It'll actually save you money, as you won't have to buy all the ingredients that go into it, and best of all it'll save you time too.

Thyme: I've brought this herb into this book as I'm currently obsessed with thyme. I luckily managed to pick up a thyme plant from the garden centre at the beginning of lockdown. It's easily interchangeable with oregano.

Tinned fish: there are so many amazing varieties of tinned fish out there to experiment with, not just tuna! They last for ages, are very versatile and healthy too.

Tinned potatoes: I started to rely on these in lockdown. They are pre-cooked and allow you to make some interesting dishes, such as gnocchi, without having to peel and cook them yourself. I have enjoyed experimenting with tinned potatoes and will continue to use them long after lockdown is over.

Toasted sesame oil: my number-one top tip for cooking Chinese or Thai food. A little drizzle at the end will give you an authentic East Asian flavour.

THE CONCEPT OF THIS BOOK

The concept of this book is to show you exactly how I use my own storecupboard ingredients at home to create delicious meals every day. My aim is to showcase a definitive collection of simple recipes that are fuss-free and can fit in with your existing lifestyle to become regular favourites.

STORECUPBOARD HEROES

Each recipe has at least one essential storecupboard ingredient and I've chosen a key hero for each dish, which is indicated by a pink star. These heroes are ingredients that often last for ages, that you can rely on at short notice, and that you have possibly even forgotten are sitting at the back of your cupboard. I have combined these heroes with everyday fresh ingredients that you're used to picking up in your weekly shop along with some frozen foods too. This is fantastic value cooking that takes no time at all.

MAKING THE MOST OF YOUR FREEZER

In this book I also look to maximise the use of your freezer, a real unsung hero for the home cook. There are so many amazing things you can pick up that cost a fraction of their fresh counterparts, from huge prawns and lovely fish fillets, to vibrant veg harvested at its peak.

GET AHEAD

As a departure from my usual style, instead of recipes for one, I have been cooking larger portions and storing any leftovers in the fridge or freezer. I have found that my own cooking at home has naturally evolved into batch-cooking as I look to reduce waste – as well as my hours in the kitchen. Family life has slowly taken over and I am relying more and more on having meals ready to warm up at a moment's notice. But if you want to cook only one portion, it is really easy to reduce the quantities. All the recipes are written in the same familiar style and format as my previous books.

WHAT TO DO WITH LEFTOVERS

Batch-cooking is also great for packed lunches, taking a home-cooked meal to work or when you're on the go. The recipes in this book will give you multiple options. Remember to store leftovers in the fridge in airtight containers and they should keep for up to three days. Food lasts for one to three months in the freezer. Always cool leftovers down as quickly as possible (within two hours) before storing. And finally, label your leftovers with the content and date, or you might find you have to guess what they are!

LESS WASTE

Due to the long-lasting nature of storecupboard ingredients, it's easy to hoard them, and this is something I discovered when lockdown started. It turned out I'd been hoarding without even knowing it! I had boxes and boxes of tins, so I set about using them up and creating my definitive collection of storecupboard recipes. To make the most of my ingredients, the first task I gave myself was to write a list of everything I already had. I then planned out my meals and bought only a few extra ingredients to supplement them. I found this method of cooking to be really economical. You can also get some great deals if you buy in bulk, which is fantastic news because storecupboard staples last for ages (which has sort of put me back in the same position as I started, as I've stocked up again). Always check what you have in the cupboard before you go shopping, and you'll not only save money but also avoid waste. Many storecupboard essentials come in recyclable packaging, so there's less waste going to landfill too.

ALL RECIPES
MAKE FOUR SERVINGS

YOU'LL NOTICE THE RECIPES IN THIS BOOK
NOW SERVE 4 PEOPLE RATHER THAN 1.

But don't worry. They still cost £1 per person. Plus, you can simply
divide the quantities depending on your circumstances, or cook the whole
amount and enjoy leftovers the next day.

MIGUEL BARCLAY'S **MEAT-FREE** One Pound Meals
MIGUEL BARCLAY'S **VEGAN** One Pound Meals
MIGUEL BARCLAY'S One Pound Meals **SUPER EASY**
MIGUEL BARCLAY'S One Pound Meals FAST & FRESH
MIGUEL BARCLAY'S One Pound Meals

THE
RECIPES

BAKED BEAN & ROASTED PEPPER SHAKSHUKA

Most people probably have a tin of baked beans knocking around in their storecupboard. Instead of beans on toast, why not give this shakshuka a try? Here, I've used a smaller pan for two.

To make 4 portions

2 x 400g tins of baked beans ⭐

1 tsp smoked paprika

1 tsp ground cumin

1 x 280g jar of roasted red peppers in oil, drained

4 eggs

Handful of crumbled feta cheese

4 slices of bread (any type), toasted

Salt and pepper

To cook

Grab a large frying pan, get it on a medium heat and empty the beans into it. Stir in the paprika and cumin, season and add the roasted peppers. Bring to a simmer then crack in 4 eggs. Either wait for them to cook on the hob, or you can put the pan under a hot grill. After a few minutes, once the eggs are cooked (but the yolks are still runny), scatter over the feta, add some cracked black pepper and serve with toast.

GREEK SALAD ORZO

When I first worked in an office, everyone used to eat these cold pasta salads for lunch. I remember feeling like a real adult eating them. Here I have made my ultimate packed-lunch salad, using orzo pasta and tangy feta cheese.

To make 4 portions

150g orzo pasta ⭐

½ cucumber, chopped

Handful of cherry tomatoes, quartered

Handful of black olives, sliced

1 red onion, thinly sliced

100g feta cheese, cubed

A few pinches of dried oregano

½ lemon

Olive oil

Salt and pepper

To cook

Boil the orzo in salted water according to the packet instructions, then drain, drizzle with a little olive oil and allow to cool.

Once cooled, mix with the cucumber, tomatoes, olives, onion, feta and a pinch of oregano, then season with salt and pepper. Dress with a squeeze of lemon juice and a drizzle of olive oil. Finish with a final pinch of oregano.

Make it vegan
To make this dish vegan, swap the feta for a plant-based cheese.

PAELLA VALENCIANA

I love the deep flavour of a chicken-based paella, especially using chicken thighs, but I like my chicken extra crispy and with a nice bit of colour. Here you have the best of both worlds.

To make 4 portions

4 boneless chicken thighs, skin on

1 large onion, diced

2 garlic cloves, sliced

1 tomato, roughly chopped

½ tsp paprika

200g paella rice

1 chicken stock cube

750ml boiling water

Pinch of saffron (optional)

Handful of green beans, sliced lengthways

Olive oil

Salt and pepper

To cook

Grab the biggest frying pan you have and start by seasoning and pan-frying the chicken thighs in a splash of olive oil over a medium heat for about 7 minutes on each side, or until golden brown and crispy and cooked through. Remove from the pan and set to one side.

Pan-fry the onion for a few minutes until soft. Next add the garlic and continue to cook for a few more minutes until it starts to colour. Add the tomato and paprika and after a few more minutes, add the rice. Stir the rice to coat it in all the flavours of the pan.

Meanwhile, dissolve the stock cube in the boiling water, add the saffron, if using, then pour the stock into the pan. Now leave the pan to simmer over a low heat and do not touch it.

After about 15 minutes, when most of the water has been absorbed, place the chicken and green beans on top for a final 10 minutes. Season, then serve.

SAUTÉD TINNED POTATO NACHOS

It's time consuming to make the perfect sautéd potatoes, as it involves multiple steps and multiple pans. So here is my shortcut using tinned potatoes.

To make 4 portions

2 x 300g tins of potatoes, drained ⭐ₛ

1 tsp ground cumin

Handful of cherry tomatoes

Squirt of sriracha

1 avocado, sliced

2 tbsp crème fraîche

2 spring onions, sliced

Handful of feta cheese, crumbled

Handful of fresh coriander, chopped

Olive oil

Salt and pepper

To cook

Thinly slice your potatoes, lightly dust with cumin and then pan-fry in batches in a generous splash of olive oil over a medium to high heat. Season and then set to one side on some kitchen paper.

Meanwhile, make your salsa by chopping your tomatoes, seasoning and mixing with a squirt of sriracha.

Place the potatoes in a serving dish and top with the salsa, sliced avocado, crème fraîche, spring onions, feta and coriander.

GOAT'S CHEESE & BEETROOT SALAD

The great thing about vacuum-packed beetroot is that there is no cooking involved, making it extremely easy to use. This recipe is based on the classic flavour combination of goat's cheese, honey and walnuts.

To make 4 portions

4 pre-cooked beetroots, chopped

200g goat's cheese, sliced

Handful of watercress

Handful of spinach

Handful of walnuts, chopped ⭐

1 tbsp honey

Olive oil

Sprinkle of fresh or dried thyme (optional)

To cook

Grab a big bowl, add the chopped beetroots, goat's cheese, watercress, spinach and walnuts, then drizzle over some honey and a little olive oil, and sprinkle over some thyme leaves. Told you it was easy!

BACON, MUSHROOMS & TARRAGON

The base of this recipe is a creamy tarragon sauce that's usually served with chicken, but here I have turned it into more of a stew to take advantage of whatever you have in your storecupboard or freezer.

To make 4 portions

500g baby potatoes (or 1 x 300g tin of potatoes), cut in half

150g smoked bacon lardons (or chopped bacon rashers)

1 onion, sliced

1 x 285g tin of mushrooms (or 300g button mushrooms), sliced ⭐

1 chicken stock cube

300ml single cream

Handful of fresh tarragon (or 1 tsp dried tarragon)

Olive oil

Salt and pepper

To cook

Start by boiling the potatoes in salted water for about 15 minutes or until cooked, then drain and set aside to cool. (If using tinned potatoes, simply drain before cutting in half.)

Pan-fry the bacon and onion in a splash of olive oil over a medium heat for a few minutes before adding the mushrooms and potatoes. Season and continue to fry for 10 more minutes until the mushrooms are cooked. Add a splash of water, crumble in the stock cube and then add the cream. Stir until the stock cube has dissolved, and simmer for a minute to thicken slightly before adding the tarragon and a splash of olive oil. Season to taste and serve.

RED ONION TARTE TATIN

This one is really easy but looks like you've spent ages making something posh. It would definitely be impressive if you made your own pastry, but there's nothing wrong with a shortcut. So, grab some pre-made puff from the freezer and you'll see that it's no effort at all.

To make 4 portions

8 red onions, cut into wedges

1 sheet of frozen puff pastry, defrosted ⭐

Squeeze of balsamic glaze

A few sprigs of fresh thyme, leaves picked and stalks discarded (or 1 tsp dried thyme)

1 egg, beaten (optional)

Olive oil

Salt and pepper

To cook

Preheat your oven to 180°C/gas mark 4. Set out a circular ovenproof dish about 15cm in diameter (or 4 small dishes).

Chuck the red onion wedges into the baking dish, drizzle with olive oil, season with salt and pepper, then roast for about 25 minutes until softened and cooked. Remove from the oven and allow to cool.

Meanwhile, lay out your sheet of puff pastry and cut out a circle 30cm in diameter. If you want to make 4 individual portions, cut out 4 smaller circles that will line the dishes with a 5cm overhang.

Add a squeeze of balsamic glaze to the onions, along with some thyme, then place the pastry on top and tuck in the sides. Brush with beaten egg if you want a professional finish and then bake in the oven for about 25 minutes until golden brown. To serve, invert the tart onto a plate or serving board.

SMOKED BRANDADE

This twist on a French classic is a great recipe to try with tinned potatoes. I have used smoked salmon for an extra kick of flavour that will transform this dish – with minimal effort on your part.

To make 4 portions

2 x 300g tins of potatoes ⭐

4 spring onions, sliced

100ml milk

A few slices of smoked salmon, chopped

Handful of grated Cheddar cheese

Olive oil

Salt and pepper

To cook

Preheat your oven to 190°C/gas mark 5.

Put a few potatoes to one side for later and boil the rest in salted water for about 5 minutes or until they are soft all the way through. Drain and then mash with the spring onions, milk, smoked salmon, Cheddar and plenty of salt and pepper.

Transfer to a large ovenproof dish or 4 small ones. Thinly slice the reserved potatoes and place them on top. Drizzle with olive oil and season with salt and pepper, then bake in the oven for about 15–20 minutes until the potatoes are golden brown.

ALOO MASALA CONES

This very simple recipe takes a handful of basic ingredients and transforms them with trusty storecupboard spices.

To make 4 portions

4 potatoes, roughly diced (or 1 x 300g tin of potatoes)

1 onion, thinly sliced

2 tsp curry powder

1 tsp ground turmeric (optional)

Pinch of nigella seeds

Handful of fresh coriander, chopped

4 mini wholemeal wraps

Olive oil

Salt and pepper

To cook

Boil the potatoes in salted water for about 15 minutes until soft, then drain. If using tinned potatoes, drain, dice and set aside.

Pan-fry the onion in a splash of olive oil over a medium heat for 5 minutes until softened. Add the curry powder and continue to fry for about 10 seconds before seasoning and adding the turmeric, if using, the cooked potatoes and a splash of water. Continue to cook over a medium heat for about 5 minutes, allowing the potatoes to disintegrate slightly so they absorb as much of the flavour as possible, then throw in the nigella seeds and coriander for a final minute.

Make a cone shape with one of the wraps and then spoon in some of the soft potato mixture. Repeat with the remaining wraps.

SUMMER CHICKEN BROTH

This is a one-pot delight where you can cram in as many veg as possible. It's true storecupboard cooking but much more fresh and vibrant than you'd expect.

To make 4 portions

Handful of fresh or frozen leeks, sliced

4 mini chicken breast fillets

1.5 litres water

2 vegetable stock cubes, crumbled

4 handfuls of any frozen, or fresh, green veg (e.g. peas, beans, broccoli, asparagus)

1 x 400g tin of borlotti beans (or any white bean), drained

1 tbsp pesto

Olive oil

Salt and pepper

To cook

Grab a big saucepan and season and gently fry the leeks in a splash of olive oil over a low heat for about 8 minutes until softened (fry for a few minutes more if you are using frozen leeks).

Next add the chicken, water and stock cubes. Simmer for about 15 minutes until the chicken is cooked through. Remove the chicken, slice it and return to the pan along with the green veg and beans, then simmer for another 5 minutes.

Meanwhile, mix the pesto with 4 tablespoons of water to make a sauce.

When the veg is cooked, serve the soup garnished with a drizzle of pesto sauce.

BLACKENED COD

Kim Kardashian apparently likes to eat black cod at Nobu (£42.50 at the time of writing). Here is my £1 version, using frozen fish fillets and a few storecupboard ingredients.

To make 4 portions

4 frozen cod fillets (or other white fish), defrosted

4 tbsp honey

4 tbsp soy sauce

4 tbsp sesame oil

1 mug of basmati rice ⭐

2 mugs of water

Sprig of fresh thyme, to garnish

Salt

To cook

Once the cod fillets have defrosted, pat them dry using kitchen paper. Mix together the honey, soy sauce and sesame oil, then coat the fish with the mixture and leave to marinate for about 10 minutes.

Meanwhile, put the rice and water in a saucepan with a pinch of salt. Cover with a lid and bring to the boil, then simmer for about 7 minutes until all the water has been absorbed and the rice is cooked.

Preheat a frying pan over a medium heat and fry the marinated fish for about 4 minutes on each side. The trick to stopping it sticking is to move the fish slightly for the first few seconds of cooking, then don't touch it again until it's time to turn. Once cooked, garnish with thyme and serve with the rice.

SICILIAN FOCACCIA PIZZA

In Italy, there's a type of pizza with a focaccia base that they sell by the gram. They just cut off a slice, weigh it and wrap it in paper for you to take home to eat. I rather like that idea.

To make 4 portions

250g strong bread flour ⭐

200ml lukewarm water

7g dried yeast

50g sun-dried tomatoes

1 garlic clove

1 spring onion, thinly sliced

1 ball of mozzarella cheese

Olive oil

Salt and pepper

To cook

Grab a bowl and mix together the flour, water and yeast along with a big pinch of salt to create a wet dough. Transfer the dough to an oiled baking tray, brush with oil and cover with a tea towel. Put in a warm place, for example near a radiator, for 1 hour to rise.

Meanwhile, throw the sun-dried tomatoes and garlic into a blender along with a generous glug of olive oil and whizz to a paste.

Preheat your oven to 190°C/gas mark 5.

Once the dough has risen, punch it to knock out the air, then stretch it out to fill the whole tray. Bake for 10 minutes. Remove from the oven, spread the sun-dried tomato paste over the top, add a sprinkle of chopped spring onion, tear over chunks of mozzarella and then return to the oven for 10 more minutes, or until golden brown at the edges and the mozzarella has melted. Season with salt and pepper and cut into big squares.

DIJON LENTILS & SAUSAGES

Lentils are a delicious and cheap storecupboard ingredient, brilliant for bulking out a meal.

To make 4 portions

8 sausages

1 onion, sliced

1 carrot, diced

1 garlic clove, sliced

1 x 400g tin of green lentils, plus the liquid ⭐

1 tsp Dijon mustard

1 chicken stock cube, crumbled

Olive oil

Salt and pepper

To cook

Preheat your oven to 190°C/gas mark 5.

Lay the sausages in a baking tray and place in the oven for about 25 minutes until cooked through, turning at the halfway point.

Meanwhile, pan-fry the onion and carrot in a splash of olive oil over a medium heat for about 5 minutes until softened. Add the garlic and cook for another few minutes. Add the lentils, mustard, stock cube and season. Add a splash more water, then bring to the boil and simmer for a few minutes before serving with the sausages.

SWEET POTATO CHAAT

This has a lovely sweet flavour and, with the contrasting combination of roasted and raw ingredients, makes for an exciting lunch.

To make 4 portions

4 sweet potatoes, unpeeled and roughly chopped

1 tsp curry powder ⭐

Handful of peanuts

1 red onion, very thinly sliced

1 tbsp honey

1 large tomato, chopped

Sprigs of fresh coriander, for garnish

Olive oil

Salt and pepper

To cook

Preheat your oven to 190°C/gas mark 5.

Coat the sweet potatoes in a good glug of oil, the curry powder and some salt and pepper, then roast on a baking tray for about 30 minutes until slightly charred around the edges, adding the peanuts halfway through to toast them.

Once cooked, tip into a bowl and mix with the onion, honey and tomato. Serve garnished with the coriander.

Make it vegan
To make this dish vegan, swap the honey for golden syrup.

MUSHROOM FRIED RICE

This is a really tasty rice dish to try out next time you're missing those familiar takeaway flavours.

To make 4 portions

1 mug of brown or white rice

2 mugs of water

2 leeks, sliced

Handful of mushrooms, sliced

2 tsp curry powder

1 carrot, cut into matchsticks

1 x 200g tin of sweetcorn, drained ⭐

4 eggs

Splash of soy sauce

Sesame oil

Salt and pepper

To cook

Put the rice and water in a saucepan with a pinch of salt. Cover with a lid and bring to the boil, then simmer for about 12 minutes, until all the water has been absorbed and the rice is cooked. Set to one side and allow to cool.

Pan-fry the leeks in a splash of sesame oil over a medium heat for about 8 minutes until softened and just starting to colour, then add the mushrooms and curry powder. Season and continue to fry for about 10 minutes until the mushrooms are cooked. Now add the cooled rice, carrot and sweetcorn and continue to cook for a few more minutes.

In a separate pan, fry the eggs in a splash of sesame oil.

Serve the rice mixture with a final drizzle of sesame oil, a splash of soy sauce and a fried egg on top.

YAKI PEPPERS

Remember my Wagamama-inspired noodles from my *Meat-Free One Pound Meals*? I had an idea to take those flavours and see what happened if I created a stuffed pepper with them – and the result was delicious!

To make 4 portions

½ mug of basmati rice ⭐

1 mug of water

1 leek, sliced

Handful of mushrooms, sliced

1 tbsp curry powder

2 eggs

Splash of soy sauce

4 peppers

Sesame oil

Salt and pepper

To cook

Put the rice and water in a saucepan with a pinch of salt. Cover with a lid and bring to the boil, then simmer for about 7 minutes until all the water has been absorbed and the rice is cooked. Transfer to a bowl and allow to cool a bit.

Meanwhile, pan-fry the leek and mushrooms in a splash of sesame oil for about 5 minutes before adding the curry powder. Season and continue to cook for 5 more minutes. Next add the rice and a splash more sesame oil, mix everything together, then push to one side and crack 2 eggs into the empty side. Once 80% cooked, scramble them and mix with the rice, add a splash of soy sauce, season to taste, then remove from the heat.

Preheat the oven to 180°C/gas mark 4.

Cut the tops off the peppers, take the seeds out and stuff with the rice. Place on a baking tray (you could use some scrunched-up foil to keep them upright), place the tops back on and cook for about 15 minutes until the peppers are cooked, then serve.

MUSHROOM BOLOGNESE

It's always useful to have a fail-safe plant-based bolognese up your sleeve for emergencies. Grab a tin of tomatoes, whatever pasta you've got to hand and that jar of Marmite® from the back of your storecupboard.

To make 4 portions

2 onions, finely diced

4 garlic cloves, sliced

4 handfuls of mushrooms, thinly sliced

1 tsp Marmite® ⭐

2 x 400g tins of chopped tomatoes

2 vegetable stock cubes, crumbled

400g spaghetti

Olive oil

Salt and pepper

To cook

Start by frying the onions in a splash of olive oil over a medium heat for about 3 minutes. Season, then add the garlic and mushrooms and continue to fry for a further 5 minutes until the garlic starts to colour. At this point, add the Marmite® and a splash more olive oil and fry for another 30 seconds to coat the mushrooms. Next add the chopped tomatoes and stock cubes and simmer for 10–15 minutes, adding a splash of water if it becomes too thick. Season to taste.

Meanwhile, cook the pasta in boiling salted water according to the packet instructions. Drain, mix with the bolognese sauce and finish with some cracked black pepper and a drizzle of olive oil.

Make ahead
Batch-cook the sauce and freeze for when you need it. You'll have a delicious meal ready in minutes!

LEMON, CREAM CHEESE & PEA TAGLIATELLE

This is a super-simple recipe that's ready at a moment's notice. Cooking delicious dishes does not have to be hard work, especially if you are pushed for time, so give this one a try.

To make 4 portions

400g tagliatelle

Big handful of frozen peas

4 tbsp cream cheese

Zest and juice of ½ lemon

Olive oil

Salt and pepper

To cook

Cook the pasta in boiling salted water according to the packet instructions, adding the peas about halfway through. Drain, but keep a mugful of the cooking water, then mix the pasta and peas in a bowl with the cream cheese, a few tablespoons of the cooking water and a big squeeze of lemon juice. Season with salt and pepper, then garnish with a little bit of grated lemon zest and a drizzle of olive oil.

EAST END PIE & LIQUOR

A proper East End pie is traditionally a puff pastry case filled with minced beef and onion, which is pretty easy to make at home. The liquor (parsley sauce) accompaniment was a bit more tricky, but I've created something similar using storecupboard ingredients that you'll probably already have at home. Why not give it a try?

To make 4 portions

2 onions, diced

400g minced beef

2 tbsp beef gravy granules

100ml water

1 x 500g block of frozen puff pastry, defrosted ⭐

1 egg, beaten (optional)

400ml fresh or long-life milk

4 tsp butter

4 tsp flour

1 vegetable stock cube

1 tsp dried parsley (or handful of fresh, chopped)

Olive oil

Salt and pepper

To cook

Pan-fry the onions in a splash of olive oil over a medium heat for 5 minutes until softened, then add the minced beef and continue to fry for 10–15 minutes until nicely coloured. Add the gravy granules and water. Simmer for a minute or so, then remove from the heat.

Preheat your oven to 180°C/gas mark 4.

Lightly oil 4 small individual ovenproof dishes (or 1 large dish). Cut the block of pastry into 4 equal pieces and roll out to fit your dishes and create a lid. Line the dishes with pastry, spoon in the filling, then cover with a pastry lid. Brush the top with beaten egg or a little of the milk (you can make a pastry decoration at this point, if you like!), then bake for about 25 minutes, or until golden brown and flaky.

Meanwhile, to make the liquor, melt the butter in a saucepan over a medium heat and add the flour, stirring well for 1 minute to cook the flour and make a paste. Now add the milk a little at a time while stirring continuously to create a creamy sauce. Crumble in the stock cube and, once dissolved, remove from the heat, season and stir in the parsley.

Serve the pies with the liquor.

ROASTED FETA & COUSCOUS

There are so many ways to cook couscous that you probably wouldn't have thought of. Here I'm roasting it in the oven. Ordinarily, this would be a bit risky, but the tomatoes give an extra burst of liquid, ensuring your couscous remains soft while getting a little crunchy on top.

To make 4 portions

2 vegetable stock cubes

2 mugs of hot water

1 mug of couscous ⭐

1 x 200g pack of feta cheese

20 cherry tomatoes

Pinch of dried oregano

Olive oil

Salt and pepper

To cook

Preheat your oven to 190°C/gas mark 5.

Dissolve the stock cubes in the hot water. Grab a roasting tin, tip in the couscous and pour in the stock. Place the feta and tomatoes on top, sprinkle with oregano, drizzle with a generous glug of olive oil and season with salt and pepper. Roast in the oven for about 20 minutes, then serve.

SPEEDY MEATBALLS

Ikea's Swedish meatballs are a classic, so here is my shortcut version using just sausages, milk and gravy granules. That's all – and you don't need to queue or feel like you have to buy any furniture to make the trip worthwhile.

To make 4 portions

8 sausages

300ml fresh or long-life milk

2 tbsp gravy granules ⭐

Pinch of fresh or dried parsley (optional)

1 tbsp strawberry jam

Olive oil

Pepper

To cook

Squeeze each sausage out of its skin and roll the meat into approximately 4 balls (depending how big you want them). Pan-fry them in a splash of olive oil over a medium heat for about 10 minutes until golden brown all over. Next add the milk and bring to the boil before removing from the heat and stirring in the gravy granules. Season with pepper and serve with a sprinkle of parsley and a dollop of jam.

PATATAS ALINADAS

This is one of my favourite Spanish tapas. It's a great recipe for using up that classic cupboard staple: tinned tuna. Don't be afraid to overcook the potatoes; they need to be extra soft so that they can take on all that flavour from the marinade.

To make 4 portions

4 potatoes (or 1 x 300g tin of potatoes), cut into chunks

1 red onion, thinly sliced

Splash of red wine vinegar

Handful of fresh parsley, chopped

1 x 150g tin of tuna, drained ⭐

Olive oil

Salt and pepper

To cook

Start by boiling the potatoes in salted water for about 20 minutes, or until they start falling apart at the edges. (If using tinned potatoes, drain and set aside.)

Meanwhile, marinate the red onions in a splash of red wine vinegar and a good glug of olive oil.

Once the potatoes are cooked, drain and allow them to steam dry for a few minutes, then mix with the onions and all the marinade. Add another glug of olive oil if the potatoes are still a little dry. Season with salt and pepper and mix again.

Allow the potatoes to fully cool, then sprinkle with the parsley and serve with the tuna.

RED ONION NOODLES

Stuck for noodle ideas? Here's one that's so easy and so tasty. Onions are always the most flavourful part of a recipe, which is why they are the basis of many delicious dishes. Here it's all onion, so it's extra delicious!

To make 4 portions

4 red onions, finely diced

4 garlic cloves, finely diced

1 tsp chilli flakes, plus extra for garnish

2 tbsp golden syrup (or honey)

2 pak choi, quartered

4 sheets of rice noodles ⭐

Sesame oil

Salt and pepper

To cook

Start by seasoning and pan-frying the onions in a splash of sesame oil over a medium heat for about 12 minutes, or until they just start to caramelise, then add the garlic and chilli flakes and continue to cook for a few more minutes. Add the golden syrup (or honey) and cook for a final minute or so, until the onions are dark and sticky.

Meanwhile, cook the pak choi in boiling salted water for about 3 minutes. Cook the noodles according to the packet instructions and then dress them in a splash of sesame oil.

Assemble the dish by dividing the noodles, onions and pak choi between shallow bowls, garnish with some chilli flakes and serve.

CUMIN-ROASTED CHICKPEAS & SQUASH

Roasting chickpeas and squash with cumin gives such a deep, intense flavour. Cumin is one of my top dried spices and is an essential storecupboard ingredient that packs a real punch.

To make 4 portions

1 butternut squash, deseeded (or 500g frozen chopped butternut squash)

1 x 400g tin of chickpeas, drained ⭐

1 tbsp ground cumin

4 tbsp plain yogurt

Handful of fresh coriander, chopped

Olive oil

Salt and pepper

To cook

Preheat your oven to 190°C/gas mark 5.

Slice the squash into half-moon shapes, then spread out on a baking tray along with the chickpeas. Add the cumin, a glug of olive oil and a pinch each of salt and pepper. Mix everything to coat, then roast for about 30 minutes until the squash is cooked.

Transfer to a plate or bowl and serve with a dollop of yogurt and a generous garnish of chopped coriander.

Make it vegan
To make this dish vegan, swap the dairy yogurt for coconut yogurt or other plant-based yogurt.

THAI PRAWN ENVELOPES

Rice noodles cook really quickly, so I always have them to hand for emergencies. Here I have created a fun way to cook them with frozen prawns to create a lovely Thai-inspired noodle dish.

To make 4 portions

4 sheets of dried vermicelli rice noodles

1 carrot, cut into strips

1 leek, thinly sliced

Big handful of frozen raw, peeled prawns

4 tsp Thai red or green curry paste

1 lime, cut into wedges

To cook

Preheat your oven to 180°C/gas mark 4.

Lay out 4 sheets of greaseproof paper about 40 x 40cm and fold up the sides to create shallow bowls. Add a sheet of noodles to each, then divide the carrot, leek and prawns evenly between them.

Add a teaspoon of curry paste to each parcel and a big splash of water, then scrunch up the sides of the greaseproof paper to make secure parcels (making sure the joins are at the top, so no liquid leaks out). Place on a baking tray and cook in the oven for about 10 minutes. Remove from the oven, give them a stir to mix the noodles and return to the oven for another 10 minutes, adding more water if needed. Once cooked, serve each with a wedge of lime.

Make it vegan
To make this dish vegan, swap the prawns for some fried tofu and use vegan curry paste.

SAUSAGE & MASH PIE

This is a comforting and crowd-pleasing dish. It's a bit quirky but have you ever tried turning sausage and mash into a pie?

To make 4 portions

4 large potatoes, roughly chopped (or 2 x 300g tins of potatoes)

1 tbsp butter

8 tinned or fresh sausages

2 onions, roughly sliced

1 tbsp flour

500ml boiling water

2 beef stock cubes, crumbled

2 tbsp gravy granules (optional)

Olive oil

Salt and pepper

To cook

Boil the potatoes in salted water for about 20 minutes until soft enough to mash. Drain, allow to steam dry for a few minutes, then mash with the butter and a pinch each of salt and pepper. If using tinned potatoes, drain, mash and set aside.

Meanwhile, pan-fry the sausages in a splash of oil in a large casserole dish over a medium heat for about 10 minutes until they start to go golden brown. Add the onions, season and continue to cook for about 5 minutes until they are nicely coloured (add a splash of olive oil if needed).

Stir in the flour and keep cooking for a few more minutes. Add the boiling water and the stock cubes. Mix it all together (add the gravy granules at this point, if using) and simmer for 5–10 minutes until a sauce has formed.

Either portion the sausage filling into 4 small pie dishes or spoon it all into one big dish and top with the mashed potato and a twist of black pepper.

ROAST CHICKEN SLAW SALAD

This is not a traditional slaw but takes inspiration from those flavours. It is the perfect recipe for leftover chicken from a Sunday roast, but if you're craving this right now, fresh or frozen chicken thighs are the answer. They can be roasted straight from frozen, in which case just add 15 minutes to the cooking time.

To make 4 portions

4 boneless chicken thighs, skin on

4 tbsp crème fraîche

4 tbsp water

1 tsp wholegrain or Dijon mustard

½ red cabbage, finely shredded

2 carrots, cut into matchsticks

1 red onion, thinly sliced

Handful of rocket

1 x 200g tin of sweetcorn, drained

Olive oil

Salt and pepper

To cook

Preheat your oven to 180°C/gas mark 4.

Rub the chicken thighs with olive oil, salt and pepper, then roast skin-side up on a baking tray for about 25 minutes (adding 15 minutes if they are frozen), making sure they are cooked through and golden brown.

Meanwhile, to prepare the salad, mix together the crème fraîche, water and mustard. Grab a serving platter and add the shredded cabbage, carrots, red onion, rocket and sweetcorn. Season the salad lightly with salt and pepper, then drizzle over the dressing. Slice the chicken and lay it on top of the salad.

TUSCAN BREAD STEW

Stale bread roasted in olive oil with salt and pepper is one of my favourite foods. It's my secret ingredient to making the best Caesar salad. In this recipe I've used chunks of roasted bread like meatballs in a rich tomato sauce.

To make 4 portions

4 thick slices of sourdough bread

2 tsp dried oregano

2 red onions, sliced

4 garlic cloves, sliced

2 x 400g tins of chopped tomatoes

Olive oil

Salt and pepper

To cook

Preheat your oven to 180°C/gas mark 4.

Tear the bread into chunks, place on a baking tray, drizzle with olive oil and season with salt, pepper and 1 teaspoon of oregano. Bake for about 10 minutes until toasted, then remove from the oven and set to one side.

Meanwhile, pan-fry the onion in a splash of olive oil over a medium heat for about 5 minutes until softened, then add the garlic and continue to fry for a few more minutes until it just starts to colour. At this point add the chopped tomatoes, season with salt, pepper and a teaspoon of oregano and simmer for about 15 minutes (adding a splash of water if it gets too thick).

Finally, add the bread, along with a generous glug of olive oil and serve.

SEAFOOD GNOCCHI BAKE

A packet of gnocchi is a brilliant time-saving ingredient to have to hand, and if you get it from the dry aisle next to the pasta, it lasts for ages. Why not grab one and try this great recipe?

To make 4 portions

2 tbsp butter

2 tbsp flour

500ml fresh or long-life milk

2 big handfuls of frozen peas

Handful of frozen raw, peeled prawns

2 frozen fish fillets

Handful of grated Cheddar cheese

1 x 500g packet of gnocchi

Salt and pepper

To cook

Grab a big flameproof casserole dish and melt the butter over a medium heat. Stir in the flour and cook for a couple of minutes, then add the milk little by little, stirring continuously, until a sauce forms.

Add the peas, prawns, fish and Cheddar, season, then chuck the gnocchi on top. Bake in the oven for about 30 minutes until cooked, then serve.

SHREDDED CHICKEN LASAGNE

Here's a nice twist on the classic lasagne from my first book, using chicken instead of beef. Chicken legs are fantastic value for money and can be kept in the freezer for up to three months. Here they are transformed into a luxurious but lighter lasagne filling.

To make 4 portions

4 chicken legs

2 onions, diced

2 garlic cloves, sliced

2 x 400g tins of chopped tomatoes

1 tsp dried oregano

50g butter

50g flour

500ml fresh or long-life milk

8 dried lasagne sheets ⭐

2 handfuls of grated Cheddar cheese

Sprigs of fresh basil, for garnish (optional)

Olive oil

Salt and pepper

To cook

Season and pan-fry the chicken legs in a splash of olive oil over a medium heat for about 10 minutes on each side. Next add the onions and garlic and cook for 5 minutes until the garlic starts to colour. Now add the chopped tomatoes along with a splash of water, the oregano and a pinch each of salt and pepper. Simmer for about 20 minutes over a medium heat. Once the chicken legs are cooked through and the meat is falling away from the bone, remove them from the sauce and shred the meat using a fork, discarding the bones. Return the chicken to the sauce.

Meanwhile, to make the béchamel sauce, melt the butter in a saucepan over a medium heat and add the flour, stirring well for a few minutes to cook the flour and create a paste. Now add the milk a little at a time while stirring continuously to create a creamy white sauce.

Preheat your oven to 190°C/gas mark 5.

To assemble the lasagne, grab a large ovenproof dish and spread half the chicken filling over the bottom of the dish. Place 4 pasta sheets on top (or as many as needed to fully cover), then spread with half the béchamel sauce and scatter over a handful of Cheddar. Repeat the layers, finishing with a handful of cheese on top.

Cook in the oven for about 40 minutes until golden brown. Serve garnished with basil leaves, if you like.

VEGAN MUSHROOM WELLINGTON

This is a vegan dream come true, perfect for special occasions. Imagine tucking into this, with all the trimmings, at Christmas. Why not grab that puff pastry out of the freezer and give this a try?

To make 4 portions

4 onions, diced

1kg mushrooms, sliced

4 garlic cloves, sliced

A few sprigs of fresh thyme, leaves picked and
   stalks discarded (or 1 tsp dried thyme)

1 sheet of frozen vegan puff pastry, defrosted

Olive oil

Salt and pepper

To cook

Start by pan-frying the onions in a glug of olive oil over a low heat with a big pinch of salt for about 15 minutes until sticky and caramelised. Remove from the pan and put to one side. Pan-fry the mushrooms in a splash of olive oil over a medium heat for about 10 minutes, adding the garlic and thyme halfway through and seasoning to taste. Once the mushrooms are cooked, return the onions to the pan, mix it all together, then remove from the heat and allow to cool.

Preheat your oven to 180°C/gas mark 4 and line a baking tray with greaseproof paper.

Lay your puff pastry sheet on the lined baking tray, then spoon the filling in a line down the middle. Fold one side of the pastry over the other and seal the edges by pushing down gently with your fingers. Lightly score the top with a knife to create a criss-cross pattern, then brush with a little oil.

Bake in the oven for about 25 minutes, or until golden brown and flaky.

Make ahead
This can be made in advance and cooked from frozen.

PRAWN & LEEK FISH PIE

Prawns are the best bit of a fish pie, so why not grab that packet of frozen prawns from your freezer and make an all-prawn pie? I've used leeks here instead of onions because they work so well with fish.

To make 4 portions

4 potatoes (or 1 x 300g tin of potatoes), roughly chopped

1 tbsp butter for the mash, 2 tbsp for the sauce

1 leek, sliced into circles

1 tsp Dijon mustard

2 tbsp flour

200ml fresh or long-life milk

2 handfuls of frozen raw, peeled prawns

Handful of frozen peas

Salt and pepper

To cook

Boil the potatoes in salted water for about 20 minutes until soft enough to mash. Drain, allow to steam dry for a few minutes, then mash with a big pinch of salt and 1 tablespoon of butter. If using tinned potatoes, drain, mash and set aside.

Preheat your oven to 190°C/gas mark 5.

While the potatoes are boiling, sweat down the leeks in a pan over a medium heat with 2 tablespoons of butter. After about 7 minutes, when the leeks have softened, add the mustard and the flour, stir well and continue to cook for a couple of minutes. Next add the milk a little at a time while stirring continuously to create a creamy sauce. Remove the pan from the heat, season, then add the prawns and peas.

Spoon the prawn mixture into a large ovenproof dish, top with the mash and then cook in the oven for about 25 minutes, or until golden brown on top.

Make ahead
Make this ahead of time and pop in the freezer until you need it.

BBQ PORK & BEANS

The trick to getting beautiful slow-cooked pork with a charred and caramelised coating every time is to do it in two steps.

To make 4 portions

2 pork shoulder steaks

1 beef stock cube

1 onion, thinly sliced

2 garlic cloves, sliced

2 x 400g tins of cannellini beans, drained ⭐(S)

1 x 400g tin of tomato passata

25ml tomato ketchup for the beans, 25ml for the marinade

1 tbsp demerara sugar

1 tsp ground cumin for the beans, 1 tsp for the marinade

1 tsp paprika for the beans, 1 tsp for the marinade

Squeeze of honey

Olive oil

Salt and pepper

To cook

Place the pork steaks in a saucepan. Cover with an inch of water, add a good pinch of salt and crumble in the beef stock cube. Put a lid on the pan and simmer gently over a low heat for 1 hour until tender. Remove the steaks and pat dry.

Meanwhile, to make the BBQ beans, fry the onion in a large saucepan over a medium heat in a splash of olive oil for a few minutes, then add the garlic and continue to fry for a couple more minutes until it starts to colour. Now add the cannellini beans, tomato passata, 25ml ketchup, the sugar, 1 teaspoon cumin and 1 teaspoon paprika, then season and simmer for about 15 minutes until thick and reduced.

Mix up a marinade of 25ml ketchup, 1 teaspoon cumin, 1 teaspoon paprika, a squeeze of honey and a splash of olive oil. Rub the marinade over the pork and leave for a few minutes.

Set a large frying pan over a medium to high heat and when the pan is hot, fry the pork for 2 minutes on each side until a lovely caramelised coating forms.

Serve the beans topped with the pork.

ACTUAL FALAFEL

I'm always making falafel with a twist, but this time I've actually made actual falafel.

To make 4 portions

2 x 240g tins of chickpeas, drained ⭐

4 tsp ground cumin

2 garlic cloves, crushed

1 tbsp flour

Handful of fresh coriander, chopped, plus extra to serve

4 pitta breads

Salad

Plain yogurt

Olive oil

Salt and pepper

To cook

First you need to dry the chickpeas by tipping them onto a baking tray and blotting them with kitchen paper. Then place the chickpeas in a blender and blitz until they look like crumbs. Add the cumin, garlic, flour and coriander, season well, then blitz again to mix.

Take a tablespoon of the mixture and firmly shape it in the palm of your hand to create a compact ball, then flatten it slightly. Repeat with the remaining mixture, making 12 falafel in total.

Preheat a frying pan over a medium heat, add a big glug of olive oil, then fry the falafel on both sides for a few minutes until golden brown and crunchy on the outside. You might need to do this in batches. Serve with pitta bread, salad, plain yogurt and a few extra coriander leaves.

Make it vegan

To make this dish vegan, swap the dairy yogurt for coconut yogurt or other plant-based yogurt.

TUNA NIÇOISE

Tinned tuna is one of the most popular storecupboard ingredients – it's great for sandwiches, jacket potatoes and my tuna niçoise salad. You could even use tinned potatoes and green beans to add more storecupboard staples to this recipe.

To make 4 portions

Handful of new potatoes, cut in half

4 eggs

Handful of green beans

1 tbsp cider vinegar (or white wine vinegar)

1 tsp Dijon mustard

Pinch of dried oregano

1 lettuce, leaves separated

1 x 100g tin of tuna, drained

Handful of Kalamata olives

Olive oil

Salt and pepper

To cook

Start by boiling the potatoes in salted water for about 10 minutes. After 3 minutes add the eggs, and then the beans for the final 2 minutes. Drain, then set the potatoes and beans to one side to cool and hold the eggs under cold running water to stop the cooking process. Peel and cut in half or quarters. Slice half the beans.

Meanwhile, to make the dressing, mix together 4 tablespoons of olive oil with the vinegar, mustard and a pinch of oregano.

Grab your serving plates and scatter over the lettuce, then add the potatoes and beans. Flake the tuna over the top. Slice half the olives and scatter over the salad, arrange the eggs, lightly season, and then drizzle over the dressing to finish.

FROZEN VEG MINESTRONE

This is an easy one, using three of my favourite storecupboard ingredients: frozen veg, pasta and stock cubes. The frozen veg gives a freshness and vibrancy that you probably wouldn't expect if I told you I was making a soup out of storecupboard ingredients. Serve with bread, if you like, to mop up the sauce.

To make 4 portions

200g any pasta

1 onion, roughly chopped

1 x 400g tin of chopped tomatoes ⭐

2 vegetable stock cubes

2 handfuls of frozen veg

Olive oil

Salt and pepper

To cook

Start by cooking the pasta in boiling salted water according to the packet instructions.

Meanwhile, pan-fry the onion in a splash of olive oil over a medium heat for about 5 minutes or until it starts to soften. Add the tomatoes, then season, crumble in the stock cubes, add the veg and simmer for another 5 minutes.

Add the cooked pasta along with a mug or two of the cooking water (depending on how thick you want your soup). Serve sprinkled with plenty of cracked black pepper.

Make ahead

This is a great one for batch-cooking. Make double the amount and have the leftovers for lunch the next day.

SHRIMP COCKTAIL BURGER

This fresh and vibrant burger is perfect for a hot summer's day. It's inspired by that 80s classic, the prawn cocktail. So grab your bag of frozen prawns and you're only 10 minutes away from this amazing burger.

To make 4 burgers

4 handfuls of frozen raw, peeled prawns

4 slices of stale bread, torn into chunks

4 spring onions, finely chopped

Pinch of cayenne pepper

Squirt of mayonnaise for the burger mixture, and a squirt for the sauce

Big squirt of tomato ketchup

4 burger buns

A few lettuce leaves

A few slices of tomato

A few slices of cucumber

1 red onion, sliced into rings

Olive oil

Salt and pepper

To cook

Defrost the prawns under cold running water, then put into your food processor along with the bread, spring onions, cayenne pepper and a squirt of mayo. Season and then pulse to get a coarse consistency. Form into 4 equal patties and then pan-fry in a splash of olive oil over a medium heat for about 5 minutes on each side (depending on the thickness of your patties).

To make the sauce, mix together a big squirt each of mayo and ketchup.

Split the buns in half and toast the inside of them under a hot grill. Place some lettuce and sauce on the bottom halves, add a burger to each one, followed by some tomato slices, cucumber and onion rings. Top with the remaining bun halves and serve straight away.

THAI COCONUT & SQUASH SOUP

This is a hearty and filling soup, using tinned coconut milk, Thai curry paste and vegetable stock cubes, all from the storecupboard.

To make 4 portions

1 butternut squash, peeled and roughly chopped (or 500g frozen chopped butternut squash)

2 onions, roughly chopped

1 tbsp Thai red or green curry paste

750ml boiling water

2 vegetable stock cubes, crumbled

1 x 400ml tin of coconut milk

Toasted seeds, chopped fresh coriander and fresh red chilli, for garnish (optional)

Olive oil

Salt and pepper

To cook

Preheat your oven to 160°C/gas mark 3.

Place the squash (including some seeds) and onion on a baking tray, coat in olive oil, season with salt and pepper, then roast for about 30 minutes until soft and cooked but not much coloured.

Remove the squash seeds and put to one side, then place the flesh and onion in a blender. Add the Thai curry paste, boiling water, stock cubes and coconut milk (keeping a little back). Blend until smooth, season to taste and serve with a little drizzle of coconut milk and a sprinkling of toasted seeds, chopped fresh coriander and chilli, if you like.

CAJUN SHRIMP & GRITS

The trick to making a sauce that clings to the prawns is to use tomato purée, which has already been reduced. You'll have a delicious plate of comforting food at a moment's notice.

To make 4 portions

1 mug of polenta ⭐S

4 mugs of water

Handful of grated Cheddar cheese

1 onion, finely diced

1 green pepper, deseeded and finely diced

3 garlic cloves, sliced

2 tbsp tomato purée

1 tsp dried oregano

1 tsp smoked paprika

1 tsp chilli flakes

Big handful of frozen raw prawns, shell on

2 spring onions, thinly sliced

Olive oil

Salt and pepper

To cook

Make the grits by mixing the polenta, water and a big pinch of salt in a saucepan and simmering for about 10 minutes until thick and creamy. Remove from the heat, then stir in the cheese.

While the polenta is simmering, pan-fry the onion and pepper in a splash of olive oil over a medium heat for about 5 minutes until softened. Season, add the garlic and cook for a further couple of minutes.

Now add the tomato purée, oregano, paprika, chilli flakes and a splash more olive oil. Fry for a few minutes, then go in with the prawns and cook for a few more minutes until the Cajun sauce starts to caramelise a bit.

Serve the Cajun prawns with the grits and garnished with spring onions.

SAUSAGE RAGU

Using sausages in a sauce is a fast-track way of getting flavour into your dish. Try to choose sausages that contain seasonings and you won't have to buy loads of extra herbs and spices. Simply leave to simmer away and it'll taste amazing – the hard work has been done for you! I know there are all sorts of rules about what shape pasta to use with what sauce, but in this case it really doesn't matter; just use whatever you have in your storecupboard.

To make 4 portions

1 onion, diced

4 flavourful sausages

2 garlic cloves, crushed

1 x 400g tin of chopped tomatoes

Big pinch of chilli flakes

400g pasta of your choice

Olive oil

Salt and pepper

To cook

Start by pan-frying the onion in a splash of olive oil over a medium heat while you squeeze the filling out of each sausage one by one into the pan. Break the filling up using a spoon and continue to fry for about 10 minutes until it starts to colour.

Add the crushed garlic and, after another minute of frying, add the chopped tomatoes along with the chilli flakes. Season with salt and pepper, then simmer for about 15 minutes.

Meanwhile, cook the pasta in boiling salted water according to the packet instructions. Drain, reserving some of the cooking water.

Add the pasta directly to the sauce, along with a splash of the cooking water and a drizzle of olive oil, then serve.

CARROT PAD THAI

I had an idea to swap flat pad Thai noodles for ribbons of carrot and it turned out great! It totally works as a low-carb alternative. Just grab a potato peeler and you can make carrot noodles really easily.

To make 4 portions

8 carrots

1 red onion, sliced

4 garlic cloves, sliced

1 fresh red chilli, deseeded and sliced, or a pinch of chilli flakes (optional)

2 tbsp honey (or golden syrup)

Handful of bean sprouts

Handful of peanuts, roughly chopped ⭐

2 eggs

Splash of soy sauce

Handful of fresh coriander

½ lime, sliced (optional)

Sesame oil

Salt and pepper

To cook

Start by cutting the carrots into thin strips using a potato peeler. The strips will vary in width, so cut them lengthways into even-sized strips.

Pan-fry the onion in a splash of sesame oil over a high heat for a few minutes before adding the garlic and chilli, if using. Just as the garlic starts to colour, add the honey or golden syrup and the carrot strips. Cook for a few minutes until softened, then add the bean sprouts and peanuts and cook for a couple more minutes before pushing everything to one side and cracking the eggs into the empty side of the pan. Once the eggs are 80% cooked, scramble them, then mix everything together. Add the soy sauce, season to taste, garnish with the coriander and serve with lime slices, if you like.

SPINACH CURRY

One of the most useful frozen foods you can buy is spinach. It has already been wilted, so a handful of frozen spinach is equivalent to about ten handfuls of fresh! Here I have bulked it out with potato to give some extra body to the dish, plus I've put a little extra TLC into the eggs to give them even more taste and texture.

To make 4 portions

4 eggs

1 tbsp curry powder, plus a few pinches for the eggs

2 onions, diced

2 potatoes, grated

2 tomatoes, finely diced

Handful of frozen spinach, defrosted ⭐

300ml single cream

A few sprigs of fresh coriander, for garnish

Olive oil

Salt and pepper

To cook

First boil your eggs for 8 minutes, then drain, hold them under cold running water to stop the cooking process, peel and cut in half.

Sprinkle the cut sides with a tiny pinch of curry powder and pan-fry them cut-side down in a splash of olive oil over a medium heat for a couple of minutes to colour a bit. Take the eggs out and set to one side for later.

Add the onions, potatoes and 1 tablespoon of curry powder to the pan, season well and fry in a splash of olive oil for about 10 minutes. Once the potato is cooked, add the tomatoes and spinach and continue to fry for a further couple of minutes before adding the cream. Simmer for a few minutes, then serve with the eggs on top and garnished with coriander.

THAI NOODLE SOUP

This recipe is super speedy. Using coconut milk is a great way to get those Thai flavours into your cooking; it adds a sweetness and fragrance that just can't be replicated any other way. If you're vegan, make sure you choose a curry paste that doesn't contain fish sauce.

To make 4 portions

2 tbsp Thai green curry paste

1 x 400ml tin of coconut milk ⭐

200ml water

Handful of tenderstem broccoli

2 sheets of rice noodles

Pinch of chilli flakes (optional)

Sesame oil

Salt and pepper

To cook

Grab a saucepan and start by frying the curry paste in a splash of sesame oil over a medium heat for 30 seconds. Add the coconut milk, water and a pinch of salt and pepper, then simmer for a few minutes.

Add the broccoli and simmer for a few more minutes, then the noodles and cook for a further 30 seconds. Serve with a sprinkle of chilli flakes, if you like.

SHANGHAI DRUMSTICKS

You can buy huge bags of frozen chicken drumsticks at the supermarket and these are perfect for making this recipe.

To make 4 portions

- 4 tbsp soft brown sugar
- 4 tbsp honey
- 8 garlic cloves, crushed
- 4 tbsp sesame oil
- 4 tbsp soy sauce
- 4 tbsp tomato ketchup
- 1 tsp chilli flakes
- 12 chicken drumsticks, defrosted if frozen

- 1 mug of basmati rice ⭐
- 2 mugs of water
- 2 tbsp sesame seeds, toasted if possible
- 4 spring onions, cut lengthways
- 1 fresh red chilli, deseeded and sliced (or use a pinch of dried chilli flakes)
- Olive oil
- Salt and pepper

To cook

Preheat your oven to 190°C/gas mark 5.

First make the sauce by mixing together the sugar, honey, garlic, sesame oil, soy sauce, ketchup and chilli flakes in a saucepan over a medium heat and simmer for about 15 minutes, or until thick and syrupy.

Next, season and roast your chicken drumsticks in a roasting tin with a glug of olive oil for about 15 minutes. Add the sauce and continue to roast for a further 15 minutes until the chicken is cooked through.

Meanwhile, put the rice and water into a saucepan. Cover with a lid and bring to the boil, then simmer for about 7 minutes until all the water has been absorbed and the rice is cooked.

Sprinkle the sesame seeds, spring onions and red chilli over the chicken and serve with the rice.

FUSS-FREE FISHCAKES

Making fishcakes can be a messy business with all the dipping and getting breadcrumbs stuck to your fingers, so I thought I would make it easier by simply pressing the breadcrumbs onto the fishcakes – and it works!

To make 4 portions

4 potatoes (or 1 x 300g tin of potatoes), cut into chunks

2 tins of salmon (about 200g each), drained and flaked ⭐

4 spring onions, finely chopped

Big handful of breadcrumbs

Big handful of salad leaves

A few slices of tomato

Olive oil

Salt and pepper

To cook

Start by boiling the potatoes in salted water for about 20 minutes until cooked. Drain, then allow to steam dry for a few minutes before mashing. If you're using tinned potatoes, drain and mash.

Add the salmon to the mash, along with the spring onions and a big pinch of salt and pepper, then mix everything together.

Form the potato mixture into 8 equal patties. Sprinkle the breadcrumbs onto a plate, season and then gently press the fishcakes into the breadcrumbs so they stick.

Shallow-fry in plenty of olive oil over a medium heat for a few minutes on each side until golden brown (you might have to do this in batches). Serve with salad leaves and tomatoes, drizzled with a little olive oil.

Make ahead
These can be made ahead of time and cooked from frozen.

ROASTED PEPPER QUESADILLAS

It's easy to roast a few peppers in the oven, but a jar of pre-roasted peppers is really useful to have in the storecupboard if you're in a rush or can't get to the shops, so feel free to sub those in.

To make 4 portions

2 red onions, sliced

2 red peppers, deseeded and sliced

1 green pepper, deseeded and sliced

1 yellow pepper, deseeded and sliced

1 tsp ground cumin

1 tsp paprika

8 tortilla wraps ⭐

Handful of grated Cheddar cheese

Olive oil

Salt and pepper

To cook

Preheat your oven to 180°C/gas mark 4.

Grab a roasting tin, throw in the onions and peppers, drizzle with olive oil, add the cumin and paprika, season, then mix everything together to coat evenly. Roast for 15 minutes.

Lay a tortilla wrap in a dry frying pan and spread a quarter of the pepper and onion mixture on top, then add a quarter of the grated Cheddar and place another wrap on top. Cook over a medium heat for a few minutes, then carefully invert the quesadilla onto a plate and then slide it back into the frying pan. Cook the second side for a few minutes until the cheese is melted, and it's done. Repeat to make 3 more quesadillas. Cut them into quarters and serve.

> ### Make it vegan
> To make this dish vegan, swap the Cheddar for a plant-based cheese.

CAULI BUFFALO WINGS

Cauliflower florets are the perfect size and shape to make this meat-free alternative to buffalo wings. I use them here in the same way as chicken. You can use frozen cauliflower instead of fresh.

To make 4 portions

1 cauliflower (or frozen equivalent, defrosted)

2 tbsp flour

2 eggs

Handful of breadcrumbs ⭐

1 tsp paprika

1 tbsp blue cheese

4 tbsp crème fraîche

1 spring onion, sliced

Olive oil

Salt and pepper

To cook

Preheat your oven to 190°C/gas mark 5 and line a baking tray with greaseproof paper.

Cut your cauliflower into florets. Grab three shallow bowls. Put the flour in one, crack the eggs into another and beat them, and put the breadcrumbs in the third. Season the flour with a pinch each of salt and pepper. Season the breadcrumbs and add the paprika and a tiny drizzle of olive oil. Dip the cauliflower florets in the flour, then the egg, then the breadcrumbs and lay them out on the lined baking tray. Roast them in the oven for about 25 minutes or until golden brown.

Meanwhile, make a dipping sauce by mixing the blue cheese with the crème fraîche until smooth.

Serve your wings with a garnish of spring onion and the dip.

SWEET PEPPER PASTA

Stuck for a quick pasta sauce? Just grab a jar of peppers and give this a try.

To make 4 portions

1 x 280g jar of roasted red peppers in oil, drained ⭐

1 garlic clove

A few sprigs of fresh thyme, leaves picked and stalks discarded (or a pinch of dried thyme), plus extra for garnish

1 stock cube (any type), crumbled

200ml single cream

400g spaghetti

Olive oil

Salt and pepper

To cook

Put the peppers, garlic, thyme and stock cube into a blender and blitz until smooth. Transfer to a frying pan and fry for a few minutes in a little olive oil before adding the cream and simmering for a few more minutes, seasoning if required.

Meanwhile, cook the pasta in boiling salted water according the packet instructions, drain, then serve with the sauce and garnished with thyme.

FROZEN PRAWN THAI GREEN CURRY

There are plenty of books that will give you a from-scratch recipe for a Thai green curry paste, but this isn't one of them. The jarred stuff lasts for ages, doesn't waste your time and costs less.

To make 4 portions

1 mug of rice

2 mugs of water

4 tbsp Thai green curry paste ⭐

1 x 400ml tin of coconut milk

200ml water (for the sauce)

1 vegetable stock cube, crumbled

Handful of small potatoes, cut in half

Handful of mangetout, 3 or 4 cut into strips

Handful of frozen raw, peeled prawns

1 fresh red or green chilli, sliced (optional)

Sesame oil

Salt and pepper

To cook

Put the rice and water in a saucepan with a pinch of salt. Cover with a lid and bring to the boil, then simmer for about 7 minutes, until all the water has been absorbed and the rice is cooked.

Meanwhile, using a wok, high-sided frying pan or large saucepan, start by frying the Thai green curry paste in a splash of sesame oil for about 30 seconds, then add the coconut milk, 200ml water, stock cube and potatoes. Season, then simmer for about 10 minutes until the potatoes are almost cooked. Add the mangetout and frozen prawns to the pan and cook for a further 3 minutes. Once the prawns are cooked, serve with the rice and garnish with chilli, if using.

Make it vegan

To make this dish vegan, leave out the prawns. You could also replace them with an extra veggie, such as aubergine. Remember to make sure your curry paste and stock cube are vegan too.

FISH & WHITE BEAN MASH

Don't have any potatoes? Never mind, grab a tin of beans and knock up some bean mash. It works really well with a pesto dressing, and don't worry if it's not totally smooth, it's supposed to be rustic.

To make 4 portions

1 onion, finely diced

2 garlic cloves, sliced

2 x 400g tins of cannellini beans (or any white bean), drained

4 white fish fillets, defrosted if frozen

2 tbsp pesto

A few basil leaves, for garnish

Olive oil

Salt and pepper

To cook

Start by pan-frying the onion in a splash of olive oil over a medium heat for about 5 minutes until softened. Add the garlic, season and continue to pan-fry for a few more minutes until the garlic starts to colour. Next add a big glug of olive oil and the drained cannellini beans. Gently fry over a low heat for about 8 minutes until the beans are very soft, then roughly mash with a fork and season to taste.

Meanwhile, season and pan-fry the fish in another pan in a splash of olive oil over a medium heat. Depending on the thickness of the fish, it will take about 3 or 4 minutes on each side to cook through.

Mix the pesto with 4 tablespoons of olive oil to create a loose dressing.

Serve the fish with the mashed white beans and drizzle over the pesto dressing. Garnish with the basil leaves.

CREAMED SPINACH PIE

I always have frozen spinach in the freezer; it's so useful to have to hand. Here I have created a quick creamed spinach and turned it into a pie.

To make 4 portions

1 onion, sliced

1 garlic clove, sliced

200g frozen spinach, defrosted

150ml single cream

100g Parmesan cheese, grated

6 sheets of filo pastry ⭐

2 eggs, beaten

1 slice of stale bread, torn into chunks

Olive oil

Salt and pepper

To cook

Start by pan-frying the onion in a splash of olive oil over a medium heat for a few minutes until softened. Next add the garlic and continue to fry for a couple of minutes until it starts to brown. Now add the spinach and cream and simmer for a couple more minutes before removing from the heat and stirring in half the Parmesan.

While the filling is cooling, brush the filo sheets with a little oil, grab a circular ovenproof dish and line it with the filo, scrunching it up at the edges to make a sort of frilly crust.

Preheat your oven to 190°C/gas mark 5.

Once the filling has cooled to lukewarm, add the beaten eggs, then spoon into the lined dish. Drizzle the chunks of stale bread with olive oil and scatter over the spinach filling. Season with salt and pepper, then sprinkle over most of the remaining Parmesan. Bake for about 20 minutes until golden brown, then serve with a final sprinkle of Parmesan.

BUTTER CHICKPEA CURRY

Butter chicken is a classic creamy curry. Here I've created a storecupboard-friendly version by adapting it a little and getting a bit inventive.

To make 4 portions

1 onion, sliced

4 garlic cloves, sliced

2 tbsp butter, plus 2 tbsp for the sauce

2 x 400g tins of chickpeas, drained ⭐

2 tsp curry powder

2 x 400g tins of chopped tomatoes

100ml single cream

1 red onion, sliced (optional)

1 fresh red chilli, deseeded and sliced (optional)

Handful of fresh coriander (optional)

Olive oil

Salt and pepper

To cook

Start by pan-frying the onion in a splash of olive oil over a medium heat for about 5 minutes until softened. Add the garlic, season and continue to fry for a few more minutes until it just starts to colour.

Add 2 tablespoons of butter, the drained chickpeas and the curry powder. Fry for a few minutes before adding the chopped tomatoes, then simmer for 10 minutes (adding a splash of water if it gets too dry). Season to taste.

To finish the curry, add 2 more tablespoons of butter and the cream. Serve garnished with sliced red onion, chilli and coriander, if you like.

Make ahead

This freezes beautifully, so why not cook double the quantity and freeze the extra portions?

FILO-BAKED CAMEMBERT

This dish makes a perfect starter. Here I've wrapped a whole Camembert in pastry, so it'll stay together in the oven (which would be your main challenge with any other cheese). It works well with either jam or onion chutney.

To make 4 portions

5 sheets of filo pastry ⭐

1 tbsp jam or onion chutney

1 large Camembert cheese

1 tsp honey

Handful of crushed nuts (any type)

Wedge of red cabbage, shredded

1 green apple, cut into matchsticks

1 carrot, cut into matchsticks

Squirt of mayonnaise

1 tsp Dijon mustard

Salt and pepper

To cook

Preheat your oven to 160°C/gas mark 3 and line a baking tray with greaseproof paper.

Lay the filo sheets out on the lined baking tray, layered one on top of the other. Dollop the jam or chutney into the middle, spread it out a bit and then position your Camembert on top. Wrap the cheese in the filo, then turn the parcel over to show the neater side. Brush with honey and sprinkle with half the nuts. Bake in the oven for about 20 minutes until golden brown and melted in the middle.

Meanwhile, make the slaw by mixing the cabbage, apple and carrot with the mayo, mustard and remaining crushed nuts. Season, then serve with the filo-baked Camembert.

CHEESE & ONION POTATO ROLLS

Here's a great veggie alternative to a sausage roll that uses tinned potatoes to make it even easier for you.

To make 4 portions

2 x 300g tins of potatoes, drained ⭐ⓢ

Bunch of spring onions, thinly sliced

Big handful of grated Cheddar cheese

1 sheet of frozen puff pastry, defrosted

1 egg, beaten

Salt and pepper

To cook

Preheat your oven to 180°C/gas mark 4 and line a baking tray with greaseproof paper.

Grab a bowl, tip in the potatoes and mash them with a fork. Season, then mix in the spring onions and Cheddar.

Cut the puff pastry into four rectangles 15 x 17cm. Add a tablespoon of the filling to each rectangle and roll up from the short end. Lay the rolls on the lined baking tray, brush with beaten egg and bake for about 25 minutes, or until golden brown.

Make ahead
These rolls can be made ahead of time and cooked from frozen.

SMOKED SALMON & CREAM ORECCHIETTE

Smoked salmon will last a bit longer in the fridge than fresh salmon, so it's a great option when planning ahead. A little smoked salmon goes a very long way in a dish like this and will build up the flavour in the sauce perfectly with almost no effort involved. I've used orecchiette pasta here, but this recipe would work fine with whatever pasta you have in your storecupboard.

To make 4 portions

400g orecchiette

1 onion, sliced

100g hot smoked salmon, flaked (or sliced smoked salmon, cut into ribbons)

200ml single cream

Olive oil

Salt and pepper

To cook

Start by cooking the orecchiette in boiling salted water according to the packet instructions. Drain, reserving some of the cooking water.

Meanwhile, pan-fry the onion in a splash of olive oil over a medium heat for a couple of minutes before adding the smoked salmon and cooking for about 30 seconds. Next add the cream, season and simmer for a minute before adding the orecchiette and a splash of the cooking water. Give it another minute, then serve.

CHEESY VEGGIE BALLS & POLENTA

A hearty plate of food using tinned cannellini beans and trusty polenta, with some feta cheese to add a bit of zing to the dish.

To make 4 portions

2 x 400g tins of cannellini beans, drained

100g feta cheese

A few sprigs of fresh thyme, leaves picked and stalks discarded (or 1 tsp dried thyme), plus extra for garnish

2 tsp flour

1 mug of polenta

4 mugs of water

2 stock cubes (any type), crumbled

200ml single cream

1 tbsp vegetable gravy granules

Olive oil

Salt and pepper

To cook

Put the drained cannellini beans, feta and thyme into a bowl, season and mash with a fork to a coarse consistency. Roll the mixture into 16 balls (about 2.5cm in diameter) then roll the balls on a plate dusted with the flour.

Mix the polenta, water and the stock cubes in a saucepan and simmer for about 10 minutes until thick and creamy.

Meanwhile, pan-fry the veggie balls in a splash of olive oil over a medium heat for about 5 minutes to get a bit of colour, then transfer to a plate.

Add the cream to the empty pan to deglaze it, then add the gravy granules. After a few more minutes, once the sauce has thickened, serve with the veggie balls on a bed of polenta and garnish with a pinch of thyme.

GRILLED AUBERGINE ROLLS & COUSCOUS

Another delicious way to serve couscous! Here I've used a griddle to get nice char lines on the aubergines but you could use a normal frying pan too.

To make 4 portions

2 aubergines

2 tbsp pesto

Handful of goat's cheese, crumbled

Handful of pine nuts

½ mug of couscous ⭐

¾ mug of boiling water

A few basil leaves, for garnish

Olive oil

To cook

Start by cutting the aubergines lengthways into 5mm-thick slices and griddling for a few minutes on each side until cooked and charred. Set to one side.

Meanwhile, mix the pesto and 4 tablespoons of olive oil in a bowl to create a loose dressing.

Add some goat's cheese, a few pine nuts and a drizzle of the pesto dressing to a slice of aubergine, then roll it up. Repeat with the remaining slices but save some goat's cheese, pine nuts and pesto for garnishing at the end.

Place the couscous and boiling water in a heatproof bowl, let it rest for about 5 minutes, then fluff up with a fork.

Arrange the aubergine rolls on a bed of couscous, then sprinkle with the remaining goat's cheese and pine nuts, drizzle over the rest of the pesto dressing and garnish with basil.

SPICY CORN RAMEN

Here I've turned a good old dependable tin of sweetcorn into the star of this ramen dish.

To make 4 portions

Pinch of sesame seeds

1 onion, finely diced

2 garlic cloves, finely diced

1 x 400g tin of sweetcorn, drained ⭐S

2 tbsp butter

1 tsp chilli flakes, plus a pinch for garnish

500ml boiling water

2 tsp miso paste

1 stock cube (any type), crumbled

2 sheets of egg noodles

2 spring onions, cut into thin strips

Sesame oil

Salt and pepper

To cook

Toast the sesame seeds in a dry saucepan over a medium heat for a few minutes until they darken in colour slightly, then put to one side.

Put a splash of sesame oil into the pan, then add the onion, season and fry for about 5 minutes until softened. Add the garlic and continue to fry for a few more minutes before adding the sweetcorn, butter and chilli flakes. Fry for about 5 minutes, making sure the garlic doesn't burn, then tip everything into a bowl.

Now pour the boiling water into the pan, along with the miso paste, stock cube and noodles. Simmer until the noodles are cooked according to the packet instructions, then serve topped with the sweetcorn mixture, spring onions, toasted sesame seeds, a pinch of chilli flakes and a drizzle of sesame oil.

FIDEUA PAELLA

Did you know that they make a famous paella in Spain using a special pasta instead of rice? Here we're going to create our own version, snapping a load of spaghetti into short lengths.

To make 4 portions

300g spaghetti ⭐

1 large onion, diced

4 garlic cloves, sliced

1 x 400g bag of frozen raw seafood

2 tomatoes, finely diced

1 tsp paprika

2 stock cubes (any type), crumbled

300ml water from a hot kettle

Pinch of saffron (optional)

Olive oil

Salt and pepper

To cook

Start by snapping the spaghetti into roughly 2cm pieces, then toast it in a pan in a splash of olive oil over a medium heat for a few minutes until it goes a golden yellow colour. Remove from the pan and set to one side.

Add some more olive oil to the pan and fry the onion over a medium heat for about 5 minutes before adding the garlic and continuing to fry for a few more minutes until the garlic just starts to colour. Season, then add the frozen seafood. Once defrosted, add the tomatoes, paprika, stock cubes, water and saffron, if using.

Once the water is simmering, add the pasta and leave it untouched for about 5 minutes until all the water is absorbed. Don't be afraid to add a splash more water if the pasta is taking longer to cook. Keep an eye on it and use your judgement, but the end result should be a bit drier than a paella and have caramelised edges.

CANNELLONI AL FORNO

It's lasagne, but in bite-sized pieces! If you don't have any cannelloni, part-cook dried lasagne sheets and roll them into tubes.

To make 4 portions

1 onion, diced

1 garlic clove, sliced

200g fresh or tinned minced beef

1 x 400g tin of chopped tomatoes

20g butter

20g flour

200ml fresh or long-life milk

2 handfuls of grated Cheddar cheese

8–10 dried cannelloni pasta tubes ⭐

Olive oil

Salt and pepper

To cook

Pan-fry the onion and garlic in a splash of olive oil over a medium heat for a couple of minutes until the onion starts to look translucent. Then add the minced beef, breaking it up with a wooden spoon. Season with salt and pepper and cook for about 10 minutes until nicely browned. Now add the chopped tomatoes and simmer for another 15 minutes. Season to taste.

Meanwhile, to make the béchamel sauce, melt the butter in a saucepan over a medium heat and add the flour, stirring well for a couple of minutes to cook the flour and create a paste. Now add the milk a little at a time while stirring continuously to create a creamy white sauce. Remove from the heat and add 1 handful of Cheddar, then stir until it melts into the sauce.

Preheat your oven to 190°C/gas mark 5.

Find an ovenproof dish that will fit all your cannelloni tubes snugly (or 2 smaller dishes), then spoon the filling into each tube, lay them in the dish and pour over the béchamel sauce. Sprinkle with the remaining handful of cheese. Bake in the oven for about 30 minutes, or until the pasta is cooked and the top is golden brown.

COD, CHORIZO & POTATOES IN A TOMATO SAUCE

You can use any frozen fish here, and you don't even need to defrost it. Plus, you don't have to p the potatoes – it all just happens in the oven.

To make 4 portions

1 onion, sliced

Handful of chopped chorizo

1 large potato, diced

2 x 400g tins of chopped tomatoes ⭐

4 frozen cod fillets (or other white fish)

Olive oil

Salt and pepper

To cook

Preheat your oven to 190°C/gas mark 5.

Grab an ovenproof frying pan or casserole dish and start by frying the onion and chorizo in a splash of olive oil over a medium heat for a couple of minutes. Next add the potato, season and continue to fry for a few more minutes before adding the chopped tomatoes and a splash of water.

Add the fish to the sauce, season, drizzle with olive oil and then place in the oven for about 25 minutes (depending on the thickness of the fish) until cooked.

PESTO SAUSAGE CASSOULET

This is a slightly lighter version of a traditional cassoulet, with a summery vibe.

To make 4 portions

8 sausages

Bunch of spring onions, roughly chopped

2 x 400g tins of cannellini beans, plus the liquid ⭐

4 tbsp pesto

Olive oil

Salt and pepper

To cook

Start by pan-frying the sausages over a medium heat for about 15 minutes until they are almost cooked, then add the spring onions and continue to cook for a few more minutes.

Next add the cannellini beans, plus the liquid from the tin, along with the pesto and a huge splash of olive oil, and simmer for about 10 minutes. Season to taste, then serve with a drizzle of olive oil.

TINNED TOMATO RISOTTO

This is the very definition of what I am trying to do with this book: use storecupboard ingredients to make great food. This recipe is just so easy and so cheap.

To make 4 portions

2 onions, diced

4 garlic cloves, sliced

1 x 400g tin of chopped tomatoes

4 handfuls of risotto rice

2 stock cubes (any type), crumbled

50ml boiling water

1 tbsp butter

Big handful of grated Parmesan cheese, plus extra for garnish

A few basil leaves, for garnish (optional)

Olive oil

Salt and pepper

To cook

Start by pan-frying the onions in a splash of olive oil over a medium heat for about 5 minutes until softened, then add the garlic and continue to pan-fry for a few more minutes or until it just starts to brown. Next add the chopped tomatoes, season and simmer for a few minutes to reduce.

Add the rice, along with the stock cubes, and stir to coat the rice. Keep simmering and stirring until the sauce has reduced a bit, about 7 minutes, and at this point add 50ml of boiling water from the kettle. Keep stirring the rice. Once the water has been absorbed, add a little more. Keep adding water a little at a time, stirring regularly, until the rice is cooked. It will take about 15–20 minutes in total.

When ready, remove the pan from the heat, add the butter and Parmesan, stir and let it rest for a few minutes before serving with an optional garnish of basil and a little more Parmesan.

SPINACH & FETA BOREK

I love the contrast in textures here between the flaky filo pastry and the soft, tangy cheese filling. This would make a great lunchbox filler and is a perfect excuse to get that frozen spinach out of the freezer.

To make 4 portions

½ butternut squash, peeled, deseeded and cubed

1 garlic clove, sliced

150g fresh or frozen spinach

100g feta cheese

8 sheets of filo pastry ⭐S

1 egg, beaten

Sprinkle of sesame seeds

Olive oil

Salt and pepper

To cook

Place the butternut squash in an ovenproof dish, drizzle with olive oil, sprinkle with salt and pepper and bake for 30 minutes.

Meanwhile, pan-fry the garlic in a splash of olive oil over a medium heat for a few minutes until it starts to colour. Add the spinach, stir until wilted and cook for a few minutes until most of the water has evaporated.

In a bowl, crumble the feta and add the butternut squash, along with the garlic and spinach. Mix the filling gently to keep a chunky consistency.

Preheat your oven to 190°C/gas mark 5.

Brush your sheets of filo pastry with olive oil and lay them out in 4 piles 2 sheets thick. Overlap the ends of each pile to create a long rectangle. Spoon the filling down the middle, roll the pastry over it to create a sausage, then coil it into a spiral shape. Transfer to an ovenproof dish. Brush with beaten egg, sprinkle with salt, pepper and sesame seeds and bake in the oven for about 30 minutes or until golden brown.

Make ahead
This pastry dish can be made in advance and cooked from frozen.

ONE-POT VEGETABLE PILAU

Turmeric turns the rice here a vibrant yellow, which contrasts with the splashes of green from the veg. Lovely! All the veg used can be fresh or frozen, and I've even come up with a shortcut: cooking it all in one pan. If using fresh veg, the recipe is exactly the same: it just takes a minute or two less for the rice to cook.

To make 4 portions

1 onion, finely diced

Handful of fresh or frozen carrots, chopped into batons

Handful of fresh or frozen cauliflower florets

1 tsp curry powder

1 tsp ground turmeric

1 mug of basmati rice

2 mugs of water

Handful of fresh or frozen peas

Handful of fresh or frozen beans

Small handful of fresh coriander, chopped (optional)

Handful of toasted flaked almonds (optional)

Olive oil

Salt and pepper

To cook

Grab a large saucepan with a lid and start by pan-frying the onion, carrots and cauliflower in a splash of olive oil over a medium heat for about 10 minutes until softened (or 15 minutes if using frozen carrots and cauliflower). Add the curry powder and turmeric and continue to fry for another couple of minutes before adding the rice, water, peas and beans.

Place the lid on the saucepan and cook for about 10 minutes until all the water has been absorbed and the rice is cooked. Fluff the rice up with a fork, season, garnish with the coriander and flaked almonds, if using, then serve.

CHORIZO TRAYBAKE

Chorizo lasts for ages, which is why it's such a great storecupboard essential to have to hand for those days when you're unprepared. Here's an idea for how to use it in a hassle-free traybake.

To make 4 portions

1kg sweet potatoes, unpeeled and cut into wedges (or 1kg frozen sweet potato wedges)

200g chorizo, cut at an angle into 5mm-thick slices ⭐S

4 red onions, cut into wedges

Handful of tenderstem broccoli

Olive oil

Salt and pepper

To cook

Preheat your oven to 180°C/gas mark 4.

Grab a roasting tin, throw in the sweet potato wedges, drizzle them with olive oil and add a pinch of salt and pepper. Roast for 15 minutes (20 minutes if using frozen) before adding the chorizo and red onions and roasting for a further 15 minutes. Finally, add the broccoli and cook for a final 15 minutes before serving.

TINNED POTATO GNOCCHI WITH ROCKET PESTO

Don't judge me, but this is by far the quickest gnocchi I've ever made. Simply open a couple of tins of potatoes, mash them with a fork, roll with flour and then pan-fry.

To make 4 portions

2 x 300g tins of potatoes, drained ⭐

4 tbsp flour

2 handfuls of rocket, plus extra for garnish

2 garlic cloves

Handful of any nuts (pine nuts, almonds, walnuts and cashews work well), plus extra for garnish

50g Parmesan cheese, grated, plus extra for garnish

Olive oil

Salt and pepper

To cook

Tip the potatoes onto a worktop, mash them with a fork, then using your fingers, gently mix with the flour and a big pinch of salt and pepper until a dough forms. Be gentle to keep them fluffy.

Roll into a few long sausage shapes about 2cm thick, then cut into 2cm pieces. Pan-fry in a splash of olive oil over a medium heat for a few minutes on each side until they start to colour, then remove from the pan.

To make your pesto, grab your food processor and blend together the rocket, garlic, nuts and Parmesan, along with a big glug of olive oil.

Mix the pesto with the gnocchi and serve with an extra grating of Parmesan, a few rocket leaves, and nuts, a glug of olive oil and some cracked black pepper.

CAULIFLOWER MAC & CHEESE

Chunky pieces of cauliflower in a traditional mac and cheese takes it in a whole different direction with very little extra effort. It's a more balanced meal and the cauliflower is not just a side dish. If you've got any frozen cauliflower florets, these can be used instead of fresh.

To make 4 portions

400g macaroni

50g butter

50g flour

400ml fresh or long-life milk

2 big handfuls of grated Cheddar cheese

1 tbsp Dijon mustard

½ cauliflower, cut into 4 thick wedges

A few handfuls of frozen peas

Olive oil

Salt and pepper

To cook

Start by boiling the macaroni in salted water for a few minutes less than instructed on the packet until al dente. Drain, drizzle with a little olive oil and leave to cool.

Meanwhile, melt the butter in a saucepan over a medium heat, then add the flour, stirring well for a few minutes to cook the flour and create a paste. Next add the milk a little at a time while stirring continuously to create a creamy white sauce. Add 1 handful of grated Cheddar along with the mustard and stir until the sauce is smooth again. Season as required.

Preheat your oven to 180°C/gas mark 4.

Arrange the macaroni and cauliflower in a large ovenproof dish, then pour over the sauce and sprinkle with the remaining cheese. Bake for about 30 minutes until the cheese starts to brown and the cauliflower is cooked through.

With a few minutes to go, cook the frozen peas in a pan of boiling water to serve with the cauliflower mac and cheese.

CURRIED EGG MAYO LETTUCE WRAPS

If I'm going to the effort of boiling an egg, then I might as well throw in a potato too. This gives the dish an extra dimension, turning it into a hybrid of egg mayo and potato salad.

To make 8 wraps

1 potato (or 1 tinned potato), roughly chopped

4 eggs

Big squirt of mayonnaise

A few spring onions, finely chopped

½ tsp curry powder

8 lettuce leaves

Handful of cress

Salt and pepper

To cook

Start by boiling the potato in salted water for about 15 minutes until soft, adding the eggs halfway through so they cook for about 7 minutes. Drain, then hold the eggs under cold running water to stop the cooking process, leave to cool, then peel.

Once the potato and eggs have cooled down, chop them and mix with the mayonnaise, spring onions and curry powder (if using a tinned potato, add at this point). Season with plenty of cracked black pepper, then spoon the filling into lettuce leaves and serve with a garnish of cress.

CREAMY MUSHROOM & LENTIL STEW

Mushrooms are one of my favourite alternatives to meat. They give this dish a hearty flavour that will satisfy your hunger even on the coldest days. I like to buy the tins of pre-cooked lentils so this dish can be knocked up at a moment's notice.

To make 4 portions

4 potatoes, roughly chopped

4 portobello mushrooms, sliced

2 red onions, sliced

A few sprigs of fresh thyme, leaves picked and stalks discarded (or 1 tsp dried thyme), plus extra for garnish

1 x 400g tin of green lentils, plus the liquid

1 stock cube (any type)

200ml single cream

Olive oil

Salt and pepper

To cook

Start by boiling the potatoes in salted water for about 20 minutes, then drain and allow to steam dry for a few minutes. Season and mash with a glug of olive oil.

Meanwhile, season and pan-fry the mushrooms, onions and thyme in a splash of olive oil over a medium heat. After about 10 minutes, add the lentils plus the liquid from the tin. Crumble in the stock cube and simmer for a few minutes. Finish with cream and simmer for a further couple of minutes to thicken. Season to taste, garnish with thyme and serve with the mashed potato.

Make it vegan
To make this dish vegan, swap the single cream for a vegan milk alternative.

CREAMY CHEESY LEEK ORZO

This super-quick recipe is what One Pound Meals is all about: short lists of ingredients and clever little hacks to create delicious food with stuff you've probably already got in your storecupboard.

To make 4 portions

2 leeks, sliced

1 mug of orzo pasta ⭐

2 mugs of water

4 tbsp cream cheese

Olive oil

Salt and pepper

To cook

Start by pan-frying your leeks over a medium heat in a splash of olive oil for about 10 minutes until lovely and soft.

Meanwhile, boil the orzo in salted water according to the packet instructions. Drain but keep some of the cooking water.

Add the orzo to the pan with the leeks, then stir in the cream cheese and a splash of cooking water. Season to taste (add lots of cracked black pepper) and serve.

TOMATO & COURGETTE PIE

The courgettes make this look pretty and intricate but think of it like a really easy lasagne; you just need to arrange the layers and the oven will take care of the rest.

To make 4 portions

2 onions, thinly sliced

4 tomatoes, sliced

4 courgettes, sliced

1 x 200g pack of feta cheese, crumbled

2 tsp dried oregano

1 x 400g tin of tomato passata ⭐

Olive oil

Salt and pepper

To cook

Preheat your oven to 190°C/gas mark 5.

Grab a big ovenproof dish and start layering in the onions, tomatoes and courgettes, along with the feta and oregano, seasoning each layer and drizzling with a little olive oil. Save some courgette slices and feta for the very last layer.

Pour over the passata, giving the dish a little shake so it sinks through the layers, then finish with a final layer of courgette and feta on top. Bake in the oven for about 25 minutes or until it is cooked and bubbling, then serve.

Make it vegan
To make this dish vegan, swap the feta for a plant-based cheese.

CHEESE EN CROUTE

This is a great recipe for after Christmas, when you've got random bits of cheese left over. It really doesn't matter what you put in the filling; any combination will work. Just remember to defrost the pastry in time.

To make 4 portions

4 squares (about 20 x 20cm) of frozen puff pastry, defrosted ⭐

4 small handfuls of random cheese

1 egg, beaten

Pinch of thyme (fresh or dried)

Large handful of green salad leaves

Pepper

To cook

Preheat your oven to 190°C/gas mark 5 and line a baking tray with greaseproof paper.

Lay the puff pastry squares out on the lined baking tray. Divide the cheese between the 4 pastry squares, placing it in the middle, and fold the edges inwards to make a raised border. Brush the edges with beaten egg, add a sprinkle of thyme and then bake in the oven for about 25 minutes, or until the pastry is golden brown and the cheese is bubbling. Season with pepper and serve with a few salad leaves.

ROASTED CAULIFLOWER TIKKA MASALA

Cauliflower is a great vegetable to use as a substitute for meat. It has the ability to char and caramelise on the outside when roasted, and this is exactly what you need when you are making anything tikka.

To make 4 portions

1 cauliflower (or frozen florets)

1 tbsp curry powder for the cauliflower, 1 tbsp for the sauce ⭐S

1 mug of basmati rice

2 mugs of water

1 onion, sliced

2 x 400g tins of chopped tomatoes

1 tbsp ground almonds

Big splash of single cream, plus extra to drizzle

Olive oil

Salt and pepper

To cook

Preheat your oven to 190°C/gas mark 5.

Roughly chop your cauliflower into bite-sized florets and lay out on a baking tray. Mix 1 tablespoon of curry powder with a generous glug of olive oil and drizzle over the cauliflower. Season, then roast for about 20 minutes, turning halfway through.

Meanwhile, put the rice into a saucepan along with the water and simmer with the lid on for about 7 minutes, until all the water has been absorbed and the rice is cooked.

To make the sauce, pan-fry the onion in a splash of olive oil over a medium heat for about 5 minutes before adding 1 tablespoon of curry powder.

Continue to fry for 30 seconds, then add the chopped tomatoes and the ground almonds and season. Simmer for about 10 minutes, stirring in a splash of cream halfway through. If the sauce becomes too thick, just add a splash of water.

Mix the cauliflower with the sauce and then serve with a drizzle more cream and the rice.

Make ahead
Batch-cook and freeze extra portions of the cauliflower tikka masala.

CRISPY CHICKPEA CURRY BOWL

This one is all about the different textures, so make those chickpeas extra crispy by letting them rest for 5 minutes on the hot baking tray.

To make 4 portions

2 x 400g tins of chickpeas, drained ⭐

1 tsp curry powder for the chickpeas, plus
   2 tsp for the sauce

1 mug of rice

2 mugs of water

1 x 300g tin of carrots, plus the water from the tin

1 vegetable stock cube, crumbled

2 tsp soy sauce

1 x 400g tin of green lentils, drained

2 spring onions, sliced

Olive oil

Salt and pepper

To cook

Preheat your oven to 180°C/gas mark 4.

Coat the chickpeas in a generous glug of olive oil and a teaspoon of curry powder. Spread them out on a baking tray, season and then roast in the oven for about 15 minutes. Set aside to rest for 5 minutes.

Put the rice and water in a saucepan with a pinch of salt. Cover with a lid and bring to the boil, then simmer for about 7 minutes, until all the water has been absorbed and the rice is cooked. Set to one side.

Meanwhile, place the carrots (plus the water from the tin), 2 teaspoons of curry powder, the stock cube and soy sauce in a blender and blend until smooth. Transfer to a saucepan, add the lentils, bring to a simmer, then remove from the heat.

Serve the curry in a bowl with the rice and top with the crunchy chickpeas and a garnish of spring onions.

Make it vegan
Simply swap the stock cube for a vegan stock cube.

TRADITIONAL CORNISH PASTIES

Recently, I was lucky enough to be in Cornwall filming a YouTube video all about Cornish pasties and how they are made. And it turns out I've been making them wrong all my life, which includes the recipe in my first book! So here is the official recipe: a great way to use frozen puff pastry.

To make 4 pasties

1 sheet of frozen puff pastry, defrosted ⭐

1 potato (or 1 tinned potato), cut into small dice

½ swede, cut into small dice

½ onion, cut into small dice

100g minced beef

1 egg, beaten

Salt and pepper

To cook

Preheat your oven to 190°C/gas mark 5 and line a baking tray with greaseproof paper.

Cut your pastry sheet into 4 circles 20cm in diameter (you can use a cereal bowl as a template).

Mix the diced potato and swede in a small bowl. Add a tablespoon or two of this mix to the middle of each pastry circle, then add a teaspoon or two each of chopped onion and minced beef. Season with salt and lots of pepper, then fold the pastry in half over the filling and either squash the edges down with a fork (not the official way) or crimp the edges by folding them over each other to look like a rope (the official way).

Transfer the pasties to the lined baking tray, brush with beaten egg, then bake in the oven for about 30 minutes until golden brown and the filling is cooked through.

Make ahead
These can be made ahead of time and cooked from frozen.

MUSHROOMS & PEARL BARLEY

This is not really a risotto or a stew or a soup, it's sort of all three combined.

To make 4 portions

1 mug of pearl barley ⭐

1 vegetable stock cube, crumbled

200g mushrooms, sliced

2 leeks, sliced

Knob of butter (optional)

Olive oil

Salt and pepper

To cook

Place the pearl barley and stock cube in a saucepan, cover with water and simmer with the lid on for about 25 minutes until cooked.

Meanwhile, pan-fry the mushrooms and leeks in a splash of olive oil over a medium heat for about 10–15 minutes until cooked.

Drain the pearl barley, retaining a bit of the cooking water, and then mix with the leeks and mushrooms. Season, then add the butter, if using, and a splash of the cooking water before serving.

Make it vegan

To make this dish vegan, simply leave out the butter and use a vegan stock cube.

CAULIFLOWER KATSU CURRY

This katsu sauce is a triumph of lockdown ingenuity. Using a tin of carrots – yes, a tin of carrots – I've created a luxurious sauce with all the defining katsu characteristics.

To make 4 portions

1 x 300g tin of carrots, plus the water from the tin ⭐

1 vegetable stock cube

2 tsp curry powder

2 tbsp soy sauce

2 tbsp flour

2 eggs

Big handful of breadcrumbs

4 thick slices of cauliflower

4 spring onions, sliced

Olive oil

Salt and pepper

To cook

Start by placing the carrots (plus the water from the tin) in a blender, crumble in the stock cube, add the curry powder and soy sauce and blend into a thick sauce. Add a splash more water, if needed, to create the perfect consistency, then pour into a saucepan and gently simmer to warm through while you make the cauliflower.

Grab three shallow bowls. Put the flour in one, crack the eggs into another and beat them, and put the breadcrumbs in the third. Season the flour and breadcrumbs with salt and pepper. Dust the cauliflower slices with the seasoned flour, then dip in the egg and finally roll in the breadcrumbs.

Pan-fry in a splash of olive oil over a low to medium heat until the cauliflower is cooked through and the breadcrumbs are golden brown, about 5 minutes on each side.

Serve with the katsu sauce and a garnish of spring onions.

CARAMELISED ONION RAREBIT

This is luxury cheese on toast. The trick here is to add a little sugar to the onions, which helps make them extra sticky, almost like a chutney.

To make 4 portions

2 onions, sliced

1 tsp soft sugar (or any other sugar you have)

100g Cheddar cheese

Splash of single cream

½ a French baguette

Worcestershire sauce ⭐

Big handful of salad leaves

Small handful of pine nuts

Olive oil

Salt and pepper

To cook

First, gently pan-fry the onion over a low heat in a splash of olive oil, along with the sugar and some salt and pepper, for at least 20 minutes. Once caramelised and dark brown, remove from the heat and set to one side.

Preheat your oven to 190°C/gas mark 5.

Grab a bowl and finely grate the Cheddar using the finest grater you have. Add a splash of cream and mix with a fork to create a paste (about the consistency of mashed potato).

Cut the baguette at an angle into 1cm-thick slices and place on a wire rack. Top each piece with a dollop of the cheese mixture, add a splash of Worcestershire sauce to each one and then cook in the oven for about 10 minutes, or until the cheese is bubbling and the bread is toasted.

Assemble the salad leaves and the rarebit pieces on a large platter, then spoon a teaspoon of the caramelised onions onto each slice. Sprinkle over some pine nuts, drizzle with olive oil and serve.

SWEET & SOUR TOFU

Yes, we're making a Chinese-style dish using tomato ketchup and tinned pineapple. This is a great example of how a few storecupboard ingredients can be used to create something totally unexpected.

To make 4 portions

2 tbsp flour

500g firm tofu, cut into cubes

1 onion, roughly diced

1 green pepper, deseeded and roughly diced

2 garlic cloves, sliced

Pinch of chilli flakes

A few rings of tinned pineapple, roughly chopped, plus the juice

Big squirt of tomato ketchup

Splash of rice wine vinegar (or white wine vinegar)

2 tbsp demerara sugar

Pinch of sesame seeds

1 spring onion, sliced diagonally

Sesame oil

Salt and pepper

To cook

Season the flour with salt and pepper. Dust the tofu in the seasoned flour and then pan-fry in a splash of sesame oil over a medium to high heat along with the onion and pepper. After a few minutes, when the tofu starts to colour, add the garlic and chilli flakes, continue to fry for a couple of minutes, then add the pineapple, a splash of the juice, the ketchup, vinegar and sugar. Stir and simmer for a few minutes to thicken the sauce and then serve garnished with sesame seeds and spring onion.

FROZEN VEG BIRYANI

You can totally use fresh veg here if you prefer. Just chuck in whatever you've got.

To make 4 portions

2 onions, roughly diced

4 handfuls of chopped veg (e.g. courgettes, aubergine, butternut squash, cauliflower, beans and peas), fresh or frozen

1 x 400g tin of chopped tomatoes

4 tsp curry powder ⭐

1 mug of rice

2 mugs of water

2 pinches of turmeric

Handful of flaked almonds

Handful of fresh coriander, chopped

Olive oil

Salt and pepper

To cook

Preheat your oven to 180°C/gas mark 4.

Grab a large flameproof casserole dish and pan-fry the onions in a splash of olive oil over a medium heat for about 10 minutes. Next add the veg, chopped tomatoes and the curry powder and mix everything together. Season to taste and simmer for another 10 minutes.

Spread the rice in a layer on top of the curry and gently pour the water over it. Sprinkle with the turmeric and flaked almonds, put the lid on and place in the oven for about 30 minutes, or until the rice is cooked. Garnish with chopped coriander, then serve.

ORZO CACIO E PEPE

Remember the trouble I had finding bucatini for the cacio e pepe recipe in the last book? Well, this time I'm using an easier-to-find storecupboard staple, orzo. This dish is also cooked in just one pan, so is even simpler. The recipe has evolved through a combination of laziness and a requirement for more cacio e pepe in my life.

To make 4 portions

1 mug of orzo pasta ⓢ

2 mugs of water

4 tbsp butter

Handful of grated Parmesan cheese, plus extra to garnish

Salt and pepper

To cook

Start by adding about 4 big pinches of pepper (it seems a lot but trust me) to a saucepan and toasting over a medium heat for a few minutes. Add the orzo and water. Season the water with salt, bring to the boil and simmer for about 10 minutes, adding more water if needed. Once cooked, you want there to be enough water in the pan that the orzo is just poking out of the top (either add water or pour water away), then add the butter and continue to simmer for a few minutes while stirring. Remove from the heat and stir in the Parmesan.

Serve with an extra twist of black pepper and a sprinkle of Parmesan.

EXTRA-CRISPY 'BATTERED' SAVELOY & CHIPS

This is something a bit different to do with noodles and really fun to make.

To make 4 portions

4 potatoes, unpeeled

1 sheet of vermicelli noodles ⭐

4 thick frankfurters

Olive oil

Salt and pepper

To cook

Preheat your oven to 180°C/gas mark 4.

Chop your potatoes into chips and boil in salted water for about 10 minutes until soft. Drain and allow to steam dry for a few minutes.

While your chips are boiling, dip your noodles in the water for about 1 minute to soften them.

Divide the noodles into 4 equal amounts and wrap them around each frankfurter. Place the wrapped frankfurters on a baking tray along with the chips. Drizzle with plenty of olive oil and cook for about 30 minutes until everything is golden and crisp. Season the chips and serve.

SMOKY FETA MELANZANE

Feta cheese (unopened) lasts for months in the fridge, so if you're in the market for a backup cheese, it's a great choice.

To make 4 portions

4 aubergines

2 onions, sliced

2 x 400g tins of chopped tomatoes ⭐

1 tsp dried oregano

1 x 200g pack of feta cheese

Olive oil

Salt and pepper

To cook

Put a dry griddle pan or frying pan over a high heat. Cut your aubergines into 1cm-thick slices, drizzle with olive oil and add a pinch of salt. Griddle or pan-fry them over a high heat on both sides until they start to char. Pick the nicest 3 slices from each aubergine and then roughly chop the rest. Set to one side.

Season and pan-fry the onion in a splash of olive oil over a medium heat for about 5 minutes, then add the chopped aubergine and the tinned tomatoes. Add salt, pepper and oregano, then simmer for about 10 minutes (adding a splash of water if it gets too dry). Remove from the heat and crumble in most of the feta.

Preheat the oven to 190°C/gas mark 5.

Grab an ovenproof dish and layer the tomato sauce and sliced aubergines like a lasagne (finishing with a layer of tomato), then drizzle with a little olive oil. Bake in the oven for about 30 minutes until bubbling. Finish with a garnish of crumbled feta, then serve.

Make it vegan
To make this dish vegan, swap the feta for a plant-based cheese and use a vegan stock cube.

BLACK BEAN DAL

A Mexican twist on a classic Indian dish using storecupboard ingredients. Dal is definitely one of the most economical – and tastiest – dishes you can make when you're eating on a budget and is perfect for batch cooking and freezing.

To make 4 portions

1 red onion, sliced

2 garlic cloves, crushed

2 tsp ground cumin

200g dried red lentils

1 litre water

1 stock cube (any type), crumbled

1 x 400g tin of black beans, drained ⭐

Big handful of green beans, trimmed and sliced

Handful of flaked almonds

1 red chilli, deseeded and sliced

Handful of fresh coriander, chopped

2 tbsp crème fraîche

Olive oil

Salt and pepper

To cook

Start by frying the onion in a large saucepan in a splash of olive oil for about 5 minutes until softened. Season, then add the garlic and continue to fry for a few more minutes until the garlic starts to colour. Next add the cumin, lentils, water and stock cube. Simmer over a low heat with no lid for 20 minutes, or until the lentils are fully cooked and have a lovely rich, thick consistency. At this point check the seasoning and add more salt and pepper if required. Now add the black beans for a final few minutes.

Meanwhile, pan-fry the green beans in a dry frying pan with a big pinch of salt. Once the skin starts blistering and the beans are cooked, remove from the heat and garnish with flaked almonds.

Sprinkle the dal with the sliced chilli and chopped coriander, dollop over the crème fraîche and serve alongside the green beans.

Make it vegan
To make this dish vegan, leave out the crème fraîche or swap it for a plant-based alternative. Remember to make sure the stock cube is vegan too.

INDEX

First published in 2020 by Headline Home
an imprint of Headline Publishing Group

1

Cataloguing in Publication Data is available from the British Library

ISBN 978 1 4722 7342 0
eISBN 978 1 4722 7343 7

Tiles provided thanks to Bert & May www.bertandmay.com
Numerous props provided courtesy of Labour and Wait www.labourandwait.co.uk

Commissioning Editor: Lindsey Evans

Senior Editor: Kate Miles
Design: Superfantastic
Photography: Dan Jones
Home Economist: Bianca Nice
Home Economist Assistant: Jenny Craig

Prop Stylist: Lydia Brun
Page Make-up: EM&EN
Copy Editor: Sophie Elletson
Proofreaders: Trish Burgess and Laura Nickoll
Indexer: Caroline Wilding

Printed and bound in Germany by Mohn Media
Colour reproduction by Alta Image
Typeset in Brandon Grotesque, Avenir, Billabong, Yard Sale

Headline's policy is to use papers that are natural, renewable and recyclable products and made from wood grown in sustainable forests. The logging and manufacturing processes are expected to conform to the environmental regulations of the country of origin.

HEADLINE PUBLISHING GROUP
An Hachette UK Company
Carmelite House, 50 Victoria Embankment, London EC4Y 0DZ

www.headline.co.uk
www.hachette.co.uk